DEBATE CHAMPION 1

The **DEBATE CHAMPION** series is a cutting-edge three-level debate curriculum bringing interactive and comprehensive debate instruction to ELLs at all age levels. In DEBATE CHAMPION, learners are immersed in the debate experience accessed through value and policy topics to activate, construct and apply schemata. ELLs engage in attentive listening, critical reading, persuasive writing and public speaking skill practices to develop effective argumentation skills. Moreover, complete debate experiences become an important tool for learning analytical thinking skills.

The DEBATE CHAMPION series uses classic Western literature, from the recommended reading list from Korea's most prestigious schools and the American Teachers' Association, and important current issues to provide a framework for debates about topics which are important to ELLs today. Summaries of the most significant works of Western literature provide a captivating and understandable context for the discussion of debate topics. These topics are then reused and tailored to apply to a current issue of interest to people today. By building upon previous knowledge and providing sufficient language input, learners with no previous experience are able to experience perfect debate flows in the Asian Parliamentary Debate and Public Forum Debate formats from the very first unit. Learners are led through the process of constructing, attacking and rebuilding ideas in explicit steps which demonstrate creating reasons and identifying appropriate supports along with planning a debate flow and evaluating the debate.

The DEBATE CHAMPION series helps ELLs learn to speak up comfortably. Research shows that debate raises the percentage of learners with confidence to express ideas from roughly thirty percent before debate exposure to approximately sixty percent after. The DEBATE CHAMPION series creates many such exposures to create more confident learners. Learners will enjoy building debates in an authentic academic learning context while participating meaningfully to become competent debaters.

DEBATE CHAMPION AT A GLANCE

LISTEN TO DEBATE

Listen to Debate serves as a warm up activity to allow learners to speak from the very beginning. ELLs observe a sophisticated illustration and make predictions to activate schema at a reduced language level. They are able to grasp the overall concept of the literature and engage sequencing skills before reading.

DEBATE LITERATURE — 1A SCHEMA CHAMPION

CHARACTER WEB

An organizer explains the identity of each character within the literature and the relationships between them to help ELLs follow the plot.

READ TO DEBATE

Practical application of the debate principles is demonstrated in the summary of a significant work of classic Western literature. The story presented in the literature allows ELLs to consider different aspects of the debate topic. It uses more advanced language to present the story and allow schema application. Information about the setting and author is included in a chart to augment ELLs' understanding.

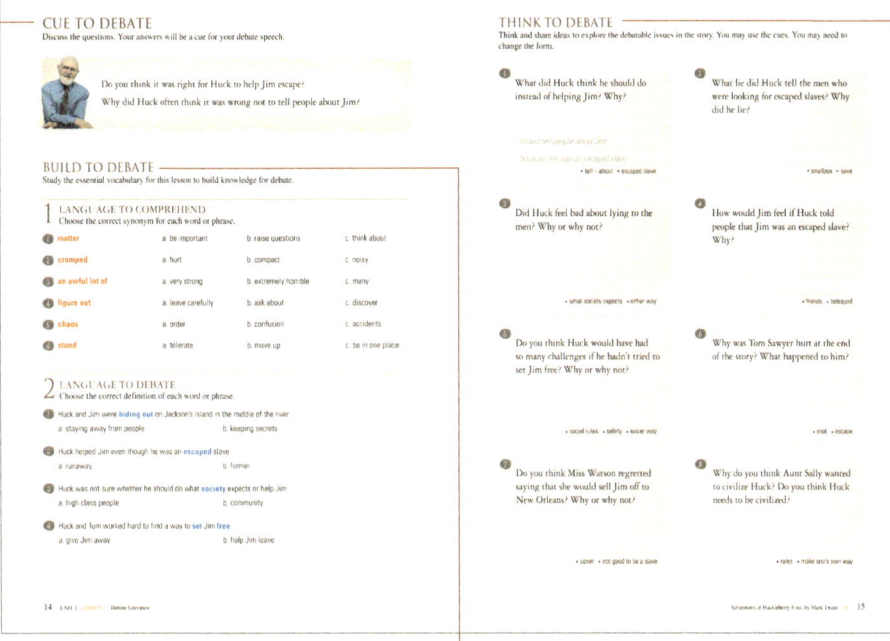

THINK TO DEBATE
In Think to Debate, ELLs are asked to consider the connection between the literature and the debate topic. By thinking carefully about these questions, they will arrive at a deeper understanding of the concepts embedded within the literature. Through thoughtful answers, ELLs will be able to develop their own view of the topic. Brief cues are provided with each question to make each response fully accessible.

CUE TO DEBATE
ELLs are given intriguing discussion questions which require a considered response to the literature. These questions encourage them to begin to view the major events in the literature from both sides of the debate in order to ignite critical thinking for the actual debate introduced in Part B.

BUILD TO DEBATE
Learners access and build important language for story comprehension and debate development. Specifically, the key language necessary to perform and interact with the debate is emphasized in Language to Debate. This accelerates ELLs' understanding of the debate themes and provides a link with the language used in the arguments.

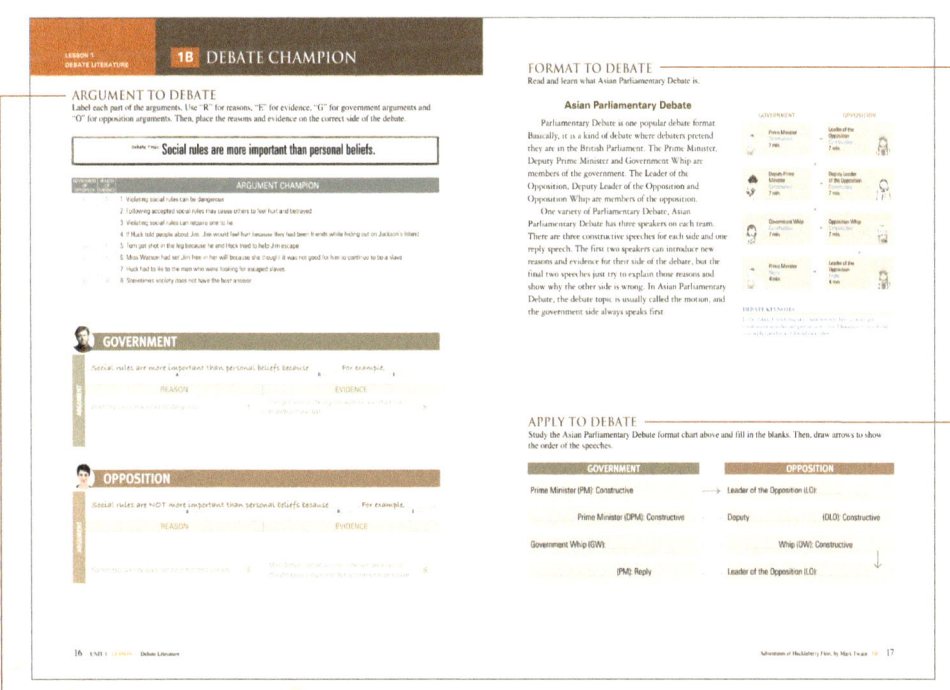

FORMAT TO DEBATE
Each of the six units contains a brief lecture over a topic involved in planning or performing a debate in the Asian Parliamentary Debate format. This lecture provides the essential metacognitive language which is required for effective debating. These topics ensure that ELLs gain useful knowledge to succeed in debate championships and tournaments.

APPLY TO DEBATE
Diverse and interesting activities check comprehension of the lecture presented in Format to Debate so that ELLs can fully apply what they learned to meaningful and practical activities. Through complete interaction with this activity, ELLs develop indispensable debate skills for future debate championships.

ARGUMENT TO DEBATE
Argument to Debate is a semi-controlled practice which allows ample opportunity to develop thinking skills by carefully considering and analyzing a selection of reasons and evidence for both the government and opposition teams. ELLs are required to identify the distinct characteristics of reasons and evidence, preparing them to build their own arguments as they advance.

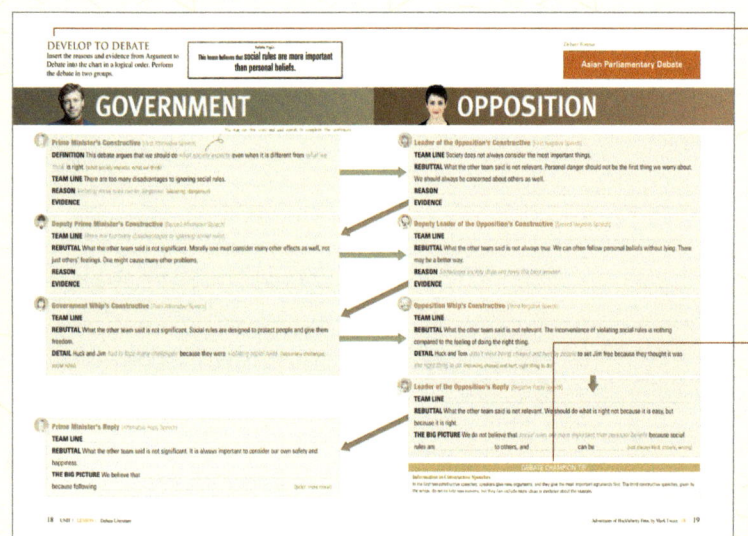

DEVELOP TO DEBATE
Finally, ELLs perform and experience the debate. Although many types of debate are used, the first debate of each unit of DEBATE CHAMPION series uses Asian Parliamentary Debate, which is the most popular debate format in Asia. ELLs are encouraged to perform the debate with full and accessible speech outlines to simulate the experience of an actual debate championship.

DEBATE CHAMPION TIP
A Debate Champion Tip provides additional information allowing learners to expand their interaction with the debates and better understand the debate process. Information is delivered in a concise and comprehensible way to create meaningful knowledge for successful debate.

DEBATE CURRENT ISSUES 2A SCHEMA CHAMPION

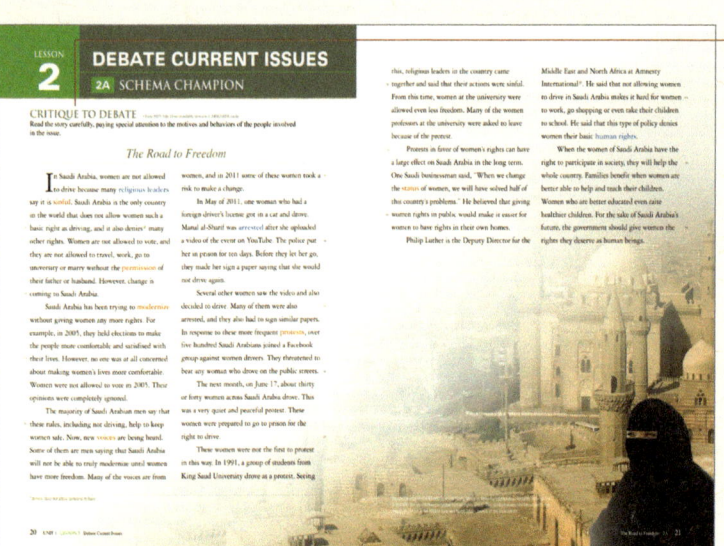

CRITIQUE TO DEBATE
Practical application of the debate principles is demonstrated in the article about a current issue given in Critique to Debate. This issue shows an explicit connection between the debate topic and the problems people around the world face today. ELLs are able to use their knowledge of society and current events to easily access the topic. Further, this article provides all the necessary information to understand the effects of the issue and speak about it intelligently.

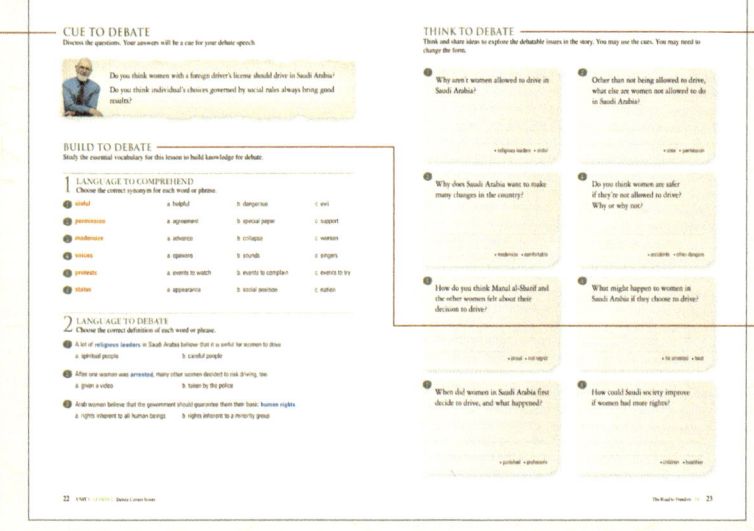

THINK TO DEBATE
In Think to Debate, ELLs are asked to consider how the debate topic can be applied to the current issue. As they go through the process of deliberation, first individually and then as a large group, they will find that they produce logical and insightful ideas. Fully engaging with this activity will enable ELLs to complete Argument to Debate successfully. Responses are made more fully accessible through the use of brief cues.

BUILD TO DEBATE
Learners access and check important language through Build to Debate. The language presented here is necessary for comprehension and also in the debate itself.

CUE TO DEBATE
ELLs are provided with a thought-provoking question to encourage them to view the current issue from both sides of the debate in order to ignite critical thinking for the actual debate introduced in Part B.

2B DEBATE CHAMPION

FORMAT TO DEBATE
The second lesson of each unit includes a lecture to explain a skill which is critical in a Public Forum Debate. These lectures allow ELLs to develop their debating knowledge and discover the best ways to apply it. By building upon previous lectures and similar lectures in previous levels, these lectures are able to deliver core information that advances with ELLs.

APPLY TO DEBATE
In Apply to Debate, ELLs can fully demonstrate their understanding of the concepts presented in Format to Debate within meaningful and practical activities. As ELLs engage in these activities, they will fundamentally expand their understanding of the basic principles of debate.

ARGUMENT TO DEBATE
In Argument to Debate, ELLs use analytical thinking skills to examine reasons and evidence and match them correctly. These semi-controlled practices build skills which will enable ELLs to produce strong arguments at all levels of education. Although many of the concepts presented here are parallel to those presented in the first lesson of the unit, the debate provides a distinct perspective guided by the current issue.

RESEARCH TO DEBATE
Research to Debate provides an opportunity for ELLs to develop critical research skills to extend their understanding of the critical issue and access additional evidence which could be useful in the debate. These research skills will become indispensable as ELLs develop into successful debaters.

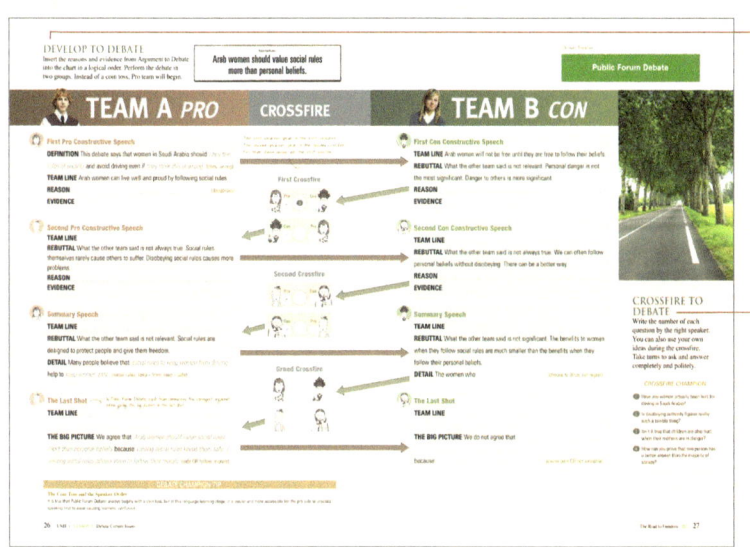

DEVELOP TO DEBATE
After identifying the best reasons and evidence, ELLs perform the debate. The debate over current issues in DEBATE CHAMPION series always uses Public Forum Debate, a popular format which is an ideal format for debating issues of interest to society. In addition to applying the content studied in the lesson to a debate, this section allows ELLs to employ their core knowledge about debate in a meaningful way.

CROSSFIRE TO DEBATE
Crossfire to Debate is intended to provide ELLs with the tools necessary to successfully and confidently participate in the crossfire sessions which are characteristic of Public Forum Debate. These questions serve both as challenges to the teams' arguments and as a springboard for further discussion.

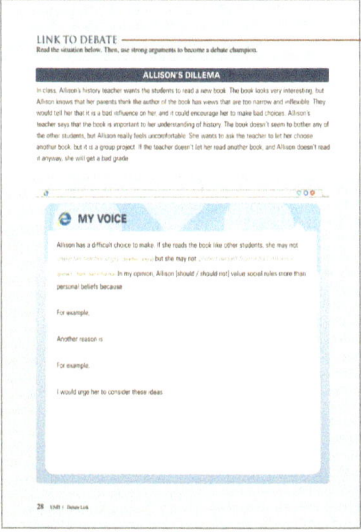

LINK TO DEBATE
ELLs have an opportunity to consider a practical situation which is related to the debate topic. This approach is meaningful as language and topics are integrated with other content-related activities to enable ELLs to apply knowledge to real-life situations.

SCOPE & SEQUENCE

UNIT	LESSON	DEBATE TOPIC
1	1 — DEBATE LITERATURE 1A SCHEMA CHAMPION 1B DEBATE CHAMPION	Social Rules Are More Important than Personal Beliefs
1	2 — DEBATE CURRENT ISSUES 2A SCHEMA CHAMPION 2B DEBATE CHAMPION	Arab Women Should Value Social Rules More than Personal Beliefs
2	3 — DEBATE LITERATURE 3A SCHEMA CHAMPION 3B DEBATE CHAMPION	We Need Help to Overcome Our Problems
2	4 — DEBATE CURRENT ISSUES 4A SCHEMA CHAMPION 4B DEBATE CHAMPION	Countries Need Help to Overcome Their Problems
3	5 — DEBATE LITERATURE 5A SCHEMA CHAMPION 5B DEBATE CHAMPION	Good Rulers Have to Experience Ordinary People's Hardship
3	6 — DEBATE CURRENT ISSUES 6A SCHEMA CHAMPION 6B DEBATE CHAMPION	Good Teachers Have to Experience Students' Challenges
4	7 — DEBATE LITERATURE 7A SCHEMA CHAMPION 7B DEBATE CHAMPION	Having More Knowledge Helps Us See the World More Clearly
4	8 — DEBATE CURRENT ISSUES 8A SCHEMA CHAMPION 8B DEBATE CHAMPION	Having More Knowledge Helps Us Make Better Decisions
5	9 — DEBATE LITERATURE 9A SCHEMA CHAMPION 9B DEBATE CHAMPION	Scientists Should Always Be Responsible for the Consequences of Their Inventions
5	10 — DEBATE CURRENT ISSUES 10A SCHEMA CHAMPION 10B DEBATE CHAMPION	Scientists Should Always Be Responsible for the Consequences of Their Inventions
6	11 — DEBATE LITERATURE 11A SCHEMA CHAMPION 11B DEBATE CHAMPION	It Is Acceptable to Sacrifice Morals to Gain Money
6	12 — DEBATE CURRENT ISSUES 12A SCHEMA CHAMPION 12B DEBATE CHAMPION	It Is Acceptable to Sacrifice Morals to Make a Living

LITERATURE TO DEBATE / CRITIQUE TO DEBATE	DEBATE LECTURE	DEBATE FORMAT	PAGE
Adventures of Huckleberry Finn, by Mark Twain	Asian Parliamentary Debate	Asian Parliamentary Debate	9
The Road to Freedom Human Rights	Public Forum Debate	Public Forum Debate	20
The Secret Garden, by Frances Hodgson Burnett	Definitions	Asian Parliamentary Debate	29
Fighting for Peace International Politics	Team Lines	Public Forum Debate	40
The Prince and the Pauper, by Mark Twain	Points of Information	Asian Parliamentary Debate	49
Beyond Native Teachers Educational Policies	Crossfire	Public Forum Debate	60
Gulliver's Travels, by Jonathan Swift	Assertion, Reason, Evidence	Asian Parliamentary Debate	69
A Web of Information Political Media	The 3Rs: Relevant, Reliable, Recent	Public Forum Debate	80
Frankenstein, by Mary Shelley	Rebuttals	Asian Parliamentary Debate	89
An Atomic Problem Atomic Warfare	Rebuttals	Public Forum Debate	100
Our Mutual Friend, by Charles Dickens	Reply Speeches	Asian Parliamentary Debate	109
Quick Cash Financial Issues	The Summary and Last Shot	Public Forum Debate	120

DEBATE CHAMPION
Real Western Literature
Real Current Issues
Real Debate Championships
1

UNIT 1
Social Rules Are More Important than Personal Beliefs

Adventures of Huckleberry Finn by Mark Twain
LITERATURE TO DEBATE

LISTEN TO DEBATE   Track 1

Listen and number each box. Take notes while you listen and tell the story using the cues. You may need to change the form.

- get an education
- fake his death
- island
- Jim

- sell Jim
- complicated plan
- be caught
- make him free

- take a raft
- get to a free state
- slave
- two liars

- Huckleberry Finn
- drunk
- take care of
- Tom Sawyer

[ ]

[ ]

[ ]

[1] - lived in St. Petersburg

- was a drunk: no one knew

- wanted to run around

| LESSON 1 | Debate Literature | Adventures of Huckleberry Finn | Asian Parliamentary Debate |
| LESSON 2 | Debate Current Issues | The Road to Freedom | Public Forum Debate |

LESSON 1 DEBATE LITERATURE

1A SCHEMA CHAMPION

READ TO DEBATE Track 2

Read the story carefully, paying special attention to the thoughts and behaviors of the main characters.

FACT FILE	Context	The story takes place along the Mississippi River in the central U.S. in the 1840s or 1850s. Most of the story occurs in Missouri and Arkansas. At this time before the American Civil War, Arkansas was a slave state, and Missouri was a border state.
	Publication Date	The book was written between 1876 and 1883 in Connecticut and New York. It was published in the U.K. and Canada in 1884 and in the U.S. in 1885.
	Author	Mark Twain was born as Samuel Clemens. He was one of the greatest American humor writers of the 1800s. He lived from 1835 to 1910.
	Genre	Satire

Adventures of Huckleberry Finn, by Mark Twain

Huckleberry Finn* lived in St. Petersburg, Missouri right beside the Mississippi River. Nobody knew where his dad was, but it didn't much **matter** because his dad couldn't take care of him anyway. Huck's dad was just a drunk. Huck just took care of himself in his own way until the Widow Douglas and Miss Watson took him into their house and tried to take care of him. Judge Thatcher was awfully nice to Huck, too.

The Widow Douglas tried hard to make Huck into a good boy. She taught him to read and write and made him study every day. Huck wasn't much used to that kind of treatment, and he wanted to be free. He wanted to run around the town and play. Lucky for him, so did Tom Sawyer, and the two of them ran around almost anywhere in the town.

After a while, Huck's dad came back. He was angry about Huck's education. He said, "You think you're better than your father, don't you, because he can't read and write? I'll take it out of you," and he took Huck away from the Widow Douglas's house as quick as you can say Jack Robinson*. Judge Thatcher tried to help Huck leave his dad, but another judge said that he'd rather not take a child away from its father.

There wasn't anything Judge Thatcher or the widow could do after that. Huck's dad took Huck off to live in a lonely cabin on the Illinois side of the river. There, Huck's dad could drink as much as he wanted. He started beating Huck pretty often, too. Sometimes, he went away for a few days and left Huck locked in the cabin alone.

*In the original text, the main character, Huckleberry Finn, tells the story from the first-person point of view as a teenager looking back at his childhood adventures.
*as quick as you can say Jack Robinson: very fast

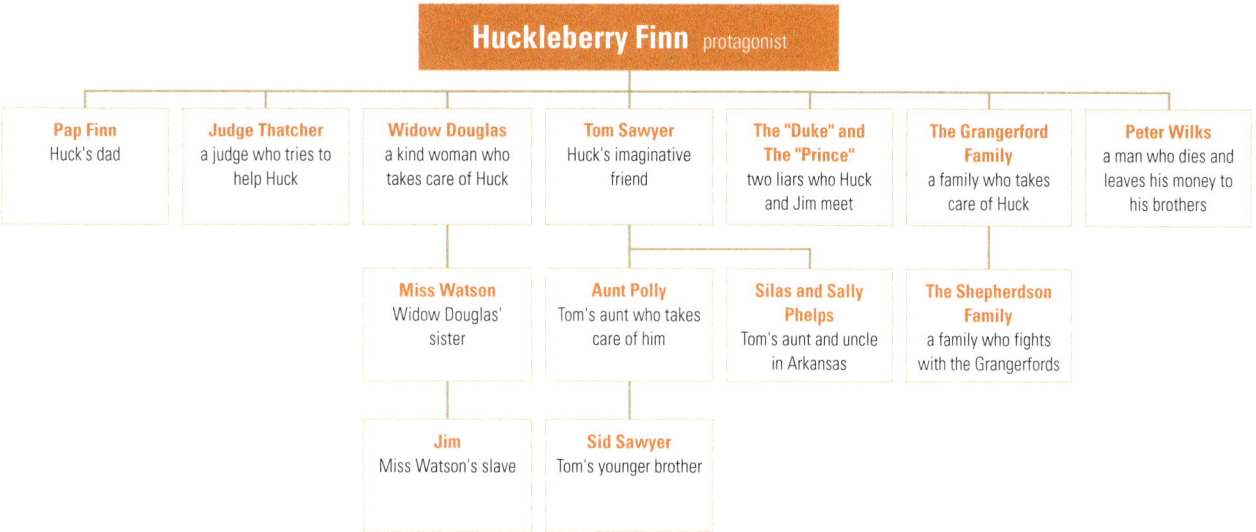

Huck got sick of it and decided to fake his own death. While his dad was gone, he killed a pig and spread its blood around. Huck knew that everyone would think for sure he had been killed. Then, Huck got into a canoe and paddled away.

He stopped to hide on Jackson's Island in the middle of the river. After a few days, Huck realized he wasn't alone on the island and met Jim. Jim was Miss Watson's slave. Huck had known him when they'd lived at the Widow Douglas' house. Well, Jim had heard Miss Watson saying that she was going to sell him off to New Orleans. He didn't want to go, so he'd just run clean away from her house. Now, there were people looking for Jim and for Huck's body. Neither one of them wanted to be found.

Jim and Huck had fun on the island, but they worried that someone would find them. Huck dressed up like a girl and went to land. A woman told Huck that she thought Jim was **hiding out** on Jackson's Island because she had seen smoke coming from the island. Huck went back and told Jim. The two of them went straight to their raft and set off down the mighty Mississippi to try to go to a free state.

Huck and Jim moved slowly down the river. They floated at night, and they hid and slept during the day. They agreed there was no home like a raft, after all. Other places seemed **cramped** and crowded, but not a raft. They felt free and easy and comfortable on their raft.

One night, the river was covered with fog. Huck went to find out where they were, but a group of men came asking questions and looking for **escaped** slaves. Huck wasn't sure what to tell the men. He knew that **society** expected him to report an escaped slave, but he also knew that Jim should be free. Finally, he lied to them. He told them that the man on the raft was his dad. Huck said he wanted help because his dad was sick with the smallpox*, and so were his mom and sister. He begged them to help. The men wouldn't go anywhere near the smallpox, though. They gave Huck forty dollars and hurried away as fast as their boat would take them. Jim was thankful because Huck had saved him. He would have felt hurt if Huck had told the truth because he and Huck had been friends.

After that, Huck got to thinking. "If you had told people about Jim, would you feel better?" he asked himself. Then, he answered, "No, I'd feel bad, just as I do now. Well, then, why should I do what society expects when I feel bad either way?" Huck couldn't answer that question, so he stopped worrying about it.

Well, the next night wasn't any better. Huck and Jim were moving down the river ever so peacefully when a steamboat slammed right into them. It threw the raft into the water, and Huck and Jim both dived under the boat. Huck came up out of the water alright, but he didn't see Jim. Huck thought he had lost the raft, and he thought that Jim was dead and gone. He had to look for some way to live.

Soon, he ended up at the house of the Grangerford family. The Grangerfords were really nice except that they kept fighting with the Shepherdson family and no one could remember why. Some Grangerford and some Shepherdson had started fighting thirty or forty years ago and now everybody in the two families was fighting.

Huck thought it was awfully bad that people in the two families kept dying, and he wanted to get away. Then, he found Jim hiding in the woods. Jim had followed Huck out of the river after the steamboat hit them, and now he was repairing the raft and getting it ready again.

After a few more days, Huck saw two men running through the woods. They jumped onto the raft. They were floating down the river with Huck and Jim before they told their story. Well, it turns out they told **an awful lot of** lies to an awful lot of people, and those people were really angry. One of them, the younger one, said he was an English duke*. The older one said he would have been King Louis XVII of France if the French people hadn't killed his father. Huck and Jim didn't want anything to do with the two liars, but they couldn't tell them to leave.

When they arrived in a river town one day, they heard that a man named Peter Wilks had just died and left a lot of money to his brothers in England. The liars told everyone that they were Peter Wilks' brothers. They took the money and planned to escape, but Huck found out. He took the money and hid it in the first place he could find. He hid it in Peter Wilks' coffin!

Eventually, the people in the town realized that the liars were not really Peter Wilks' brothers. They decided to hang them, but the "duke" and the "prince" got away. They ran for the raft and arrived just as Huck and Jim were leaving. Huck and Jim were mighty disappointed to see them, but they tried not to

---

*smallpox: an infectious disease causing fever and often death
*duke: a powerful person in England

act like it.

A few days later, Huck got separated from Jim and the liars. Then, the liars told a farmer that Jim was an escaped slave and sold him to the farmer. The farmer was planning to keep Jim locked up safe until his owner came. When Huck found out, he hurried to the farm.

When he got to the farm, a woman ran out of the house and cried, "Is that you?"

Without thinking, Huck answered, "Yes, ma'am," and then he had to **figure out** who she was. At first, he was really confused, but then he figured out that the woman thought he was Tom Sawyer. Huck had somehow ended up at the house of Tom Sawyer's aunt and uncle, Silas and Sally Phelps. The Phelps family all thought that Huck was Tom Sawyer, and Huck didn't bother to correct them.

A few hours later, Huck saw Tom on the way to his aunt's house. Huck told Tom the story, and they quickly made a plan. Huck went back to the house and lived as Tom Sawyer. The real Tom Sawyer came a little later and said he was his little brother, Sid Sawyer.

Huck and Tom then made a big plan to **set** Jim **free**. They made it as difficult as possible so that Jim could become really famous. Tom said, "Sometimes the people who are supposed to put difficulties in the way don't do it, and you have to think of all the difficulties yourself. There's more honor in getting him out through a lot of difficulties and dangers like that."

Huck and Tom caused a lot of **chaos** around the Phelps' house for weeks, and Aunt Sally was really upset by all the trouble. Finally, the two boys dug Jim out, and all three of them ran away. As they were running, somebody saw them and shot Tom in the leg. They had to stop and get a doctor, and the doctor found out about Jim. After that, they were all back at the Phelps', and Jim was locked up again.

The next morning, Tom told them that Jim had been free all along. That was because of Miss Watson dying and writing in her will that Jim should be free. She thought it wasn't good for Jim to be a slave. Tom just wanted to have fun, and he'd planned to give Jim some money.

A little later, Tom's Aunt Polly came down from St. Petersburg. When she walked in, she immediately told Aunt Sally that she'd been deceived. Aunt Sally hadn't been taking care of Tom and Sid, as she thought. She'd been taking care of Huck and Tom.

Well, all was forgiven, and Aunt Sally said she would take care of Huck. She was pretty sure she could civilize* him. Huck said he couldn't **stand** that. He'd been there before. He decided to go West before everyone else did.

*civilize: educate or improve

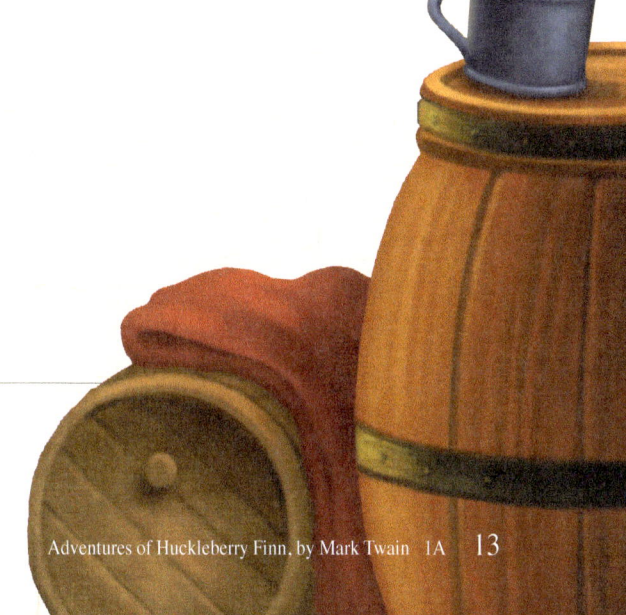

CUE TO DEBATE

Discuss the questions. Your answers will be a cue for your debate speech.

Do you think it was right for Huck to help Jim escape?

Why did Huck often think it was wrong not to tell people about Jim?

BUILD TO DEBATE

Study the essential vocabulary for this lesson to build knowledge for debate.

1 LANGUAGE TO COMPREHEND
Choose the correct synonym for each word or phrase.

1. **matter**	a. be important	b. raise questions	c. think about
2. **cramped**	a. hurt	b. compact	c. noisy
3. **an awful lot of**	a. very strong	b. extremely horrible	c. many
4. **figure out**	a. leave carefully	b. ask about	c. discover
5. **chaos**	a. order	b. confusion	c. accidents
6. **stand**	a. tolerate	b. move up	c. be in one place

2 LANGUAGE TO DEBATE
Choose the correct definition of each word or phrase.

1. Huck and Jim were **hiding out** on Jackson's Island in the middle of the river.
   a. staying away from people   b. keeping secrets

2. Huck helped Jim even though he was an **escaped** slave.
   a. runaway   b. former

3. Huck was not sure whether he should do what **society** expects or help Jim.
   a. high class people   b. community

4. Huck and Tom worked hard to find a way to **set** Jim **free**.
   a. give Jim away   b. help Jim leave

THINK TO DEBATE

Think and share ideas to explore the debatable issues in the story. You may use the cues. You may need to change the form.

1. What did Huck think he should do instead of helping Jim? Why?

- should tell people about Jim
- because Jim was an escaped slave

• tell ~ about • escaped slave

2. What lie did Huck tell the men who were looking for escaped slaves? Why did he lie?

• smallpox • save

3. Did Huck feel bad about lying to the men? Why or why not?

• what society expects • either way

4. How would Jim feel if Huck told people that Jim was an escaped slave? Why?

• friends • betrayed

5. Do you think Huck would have had so many challenges if he hadn't tried to set Jim free? Why or why not?

• social rules • safety • easier way

6. Why was Tom Sawyer hurt at the end of the story? What happened to him?

• shot • escape

7. Do you think Miss Watson regretted saying that she would sell Jim off to New Orleans? Why or why not?

• upset • not good to be a slave

8. Why do you think Aunt Sally wanted to civilize Huck? Do you think Huck needs to be civilized?

• rules • make one's own way

LESSON 1
DEBATE LITERATURE

1B DEBATE CHAMPION

ARGUMENT TO DEBATE

Label each part of the arguments. Use "R" for reasons, "E" for evidence, "G" for government arguments and "O" for opposition arguments. Then, place the reasons and evidence on the correct side of the debate.

Debate Topic: Social rules are more important than personal beliefs.

GOVERNMENT OR OPPOSITION	REASON OR EVIDENCE	ARGUMENT CHAMPION
G	R	1. Violating social rules can be dangerous.
		2. Following accepted social rules may cause others to feel hurt and betrayed.
		3. Violating social rules can require one to lie.
		4. If Huck told people about Jim, Jim would feel hurt because they had been friends while hiding out on Jackson's Island.
G	E	5. Tom got shot in the leg because he and Huck tried to help Jim escape.
O	E	6. Miss Watson had set Jim free in her will because she thought it was not good for him to continue to be a slave.
		7. Huck had to lie to the men who were looking for escaped slaves.
O	R	8. Sometimes society does not have the best answer.

GOVERNMENT

Social rules are more important than personal beliefs because _____. For example, _____.
(**A**ssertion) (**R**eason) (**E**vidence)

REASON		EVIDENCE	
Violating social rules can be dangerous.	1	Tom got shot in the leg because he and Huck tried to help Jim escape.	5

OPPOSITION

Social rules are NOT more important than personal beliefs because _____. For example, _____.
(**A**ssertion) (**R**eason) (**E**vidence)

REASON		EVIDENCE	
Sometimes society does not have the best answer.	8	Miss Watson had set Jim free in her will because she thought it was not good for him to continue to be a slave.	6

FORMAT TO DEBATE
Read and learn what Asian Parliamentary Debate is.

Asian Parliamentary Debate

Parliamentary Debate is one popular debate format. Basically, it is a kind of debate where debaters pretend they are in the British Parliament. The Prime Minister, Deputy Prime Minister and Government Whip are members of the government. The Leader of the Opposition, Deputy Leader of the Opposition and Opposition Whip are members of the opposition.

One variety of Parliamentary Debate, Asian Parliamentary Debate has three speakers on each team. There are three constructive speeches for each side and one reply speech. The first two speakers can introduce new reasons and evidence for their side of the debate, but the final two speeches just try to explain those reasons and show why the other side is wrong. In Asian Parliamentary Debate, the debate topic is usually called the motion, and the government side always speaks first.

DEBATE KEYNOTES

In the debate format diagram, characters who have a sword give constructive speeches and provide new ideas. Characters with a shield give reply speeches and defend their ideas.

APPLY TO DEBATE
Study the Asian Parliamentary Debate format chart above and fill in the blanks. Then, draw arrows to show the order of the speeches.

GOVERNMENT		OPPOSITION
Prime Minister (PM): Constructive	⟶	Leader of the Opposition (LO): _____
_____ Prime Minister (DPM): Constructive		Deputy _____ (DLO): Constructive
Government Whip (GW): _____		_____ Whip (OW): Constructive
_____ (PM): Reply		Leader of the Opposition (LO): _____

DEVELOP TO DEBATE

Insert the reasons and evidence from Argument to Debate into the chart in a logical order. Perform the debate in two groups.

Debate Topic: This house believes that **social rules are more important than personal beliefs.**

GOVERNMENT

You may use the cues and add words to complete the sentences.

Prime Minister's Constructive [First Affirmative Speech]

DEFINITION This debate argues that we should do *what society expects* even when it is different from *what we think* is right. (what society expects, what we think)

TEAM LINE There are too many disadvantages to ignoring social rules.

REASON *Violating social rules can be dangerous.* (violating, dangerous)

EVIDENCE _____

Deputy Prime Minister's Constructive [Second Affirmative Speech]

TEAM LINE *There are too many disadvantages to ignoring social rules.*

REBUTTAL What the other team said is not significant. Morally one must consider many other effects as well, not just others' feelings. One might cause many other problems.

REASON _____

EVIDENCE _____

Government Whip's Constructive [Third Affirmative Speech]

TEAM LINE _____

REBUTTAL What the other team said is not significant. Social rules are designed to protect people and give them freedom.

DETAIL Huck and Jim *had to face many challenges* because they were *violating social rules.* (face many challenges, social rules)

Prime Minister's Reply [Affirmative Reply Speech]

TEAM LINE _____

REBUTTAL What the other team said is not significant. It is always important to consider our own safety and happiness.

THE BIG PICTURE We believe that _____

because following _____ (safer, more moral)

18 UNIT 1 LESSON 1 Debate Literature

Debate Format

Asian Parliamentary Debate

OPPOSITION

Leader of the Opposition's Constructive [First Negative Speech]

TEAM LINE Society does not always consider the most important things.

REBUTTAL What the other team said is not relevant. Personal danger should not be the first thing we worry about. We should always be concerned about others as well.

REASON

EVIDENCE

Deputy Leader of the Opposition's Constructive [Second Negative Speech]

TEAM LINE

REBUTTAL What the other team said is not always true. We can often follow personal beliefs without lying. There may be a better way.

REASON *Sometimes society does not have the best answer.*

EVIDENCE

Opposition Whip's Constructive [Third Negative Speech]

TEAM LINE

REBUTTAL What the other team said is not relevant. The inconvenience of violating social rules is nothing compared to the feeling of doing the right thing.

DETAIL Huck and Tom *didn't mind being chased and hurt by people* to set Jim free because they thought it was *the right thing to do.* (not mind, chased and hurt, right thing to do)

Leader of the Opposition's Reply [Negative Reply Speech]

TEAM LINE

REBUTTAL What the other team said is not relevant. We should do what is right not because it is easy, but because it is right.

THE BIG PICTURE We do not believe that *social rules are more important than personal beliefs* because social rules are _____ to others, and _____ can be _____ (not always kind, society, wrong)

DEBATE CHAMPION TIP

Information in Constructive Speeches

In the first two constructive speeches, speakers give new arguments, and they give the most important agruments first. The third constructive speeches, given by the whips, do not include new reasons, but they can include more ideas or evidence about the reasons.

LESSON 2
DEBATE CURRENT ISSUES
2A SCHEMA CHAMPION

CRITIQUE TO DEBATE   • Free MP3 File Downloadable @www.LARRABEE.co.kr

Read the story carefully, paying special attention to the motives and behaviors of the people involved in the issue.

The Road to Freedom

In Saudi Arabia, women are not allowed to drive because many **religious leaders** say it is **sinful**. Saudi Arabia is the only country in the world that does not allow women such a basic right as driving, and it also denies* many other rights. Women are not allowed to vote, and they are not allowed to travel, work, go to university or marry without the **permission** of their father or husband. However, change is coming to Saudi Arabia.

Saudi Arabia has been trying to **modernize** without giving women any more rights. For example, in 2005, they held elections to make the people more comfortable and satisfised with their lives. However, no one was at all concerned about making women's lives more comfortable. Women were not allowed to vote in 2005. Their opinions were completely ignored.

The majority of Saudi Arabian men say that these rules, including not driving, help to keep women safe. Now, new **voices** are being heard. Some of them are men saying that Saudi Arabia will not be able to truly modernize until women have more freedom. Many of the voices are from women, and in 2011 some of these women took a risk to make a change.

In May of 2011, one woman who had a foreign driver's license got in a car and drove. Manal al-Sharif was **arrested** after she uploaded a video of the event on YouTube. The police put her in prison for ten days. Before they let her go, they made her sign a paper saying that she would not drive again.

Several other women saw the video and also decided to drive. Many of them were also arrested, and they also had to sign similar papers. In response to these more frequent **protests**, over five hundred Saudi Arabians joined a Facebook group against women drivers. They threatened to beat any woman who drove on the public streets.

The next month, on June 17, about thirty or forty women across Saudi Arabia drove. This was a very quiet and peaceful protest. These women were prepared to go to prison for the right to drive.

These women were not the first to protest in this way. In 1991, a group of students from King Saud University drove as a protest. Seeing

*denies: does not allow someone to have

this, religious leaders in the country came together and said that their actions were sinful. From this time, women at the university were allowed even less freedom. Many of the women professors at the university were asked to leave because of the protest.

Protests in favor of women's rights can have a large effect on Saudi Arabia in the long term. One Saudi businessman said, "When we change the **status** of women, we will have solved half of this country's problems." He believed that giving women rights in public would make it easier for women to have rights in their own homes.

Philip Luther is the Deputy Director for the Middle East and North Africa at Amnesty International*. He said that not allowing women to drive in Saudi Arabia makes it hard for women to work, go shopping or even take their children to school. He said that this type of policy denies women their basic **human rights**.

When the women of Saudi Arabia have the right to participate in society, they will help the whole country. Families benefit when women are better able to help and teach their children. Women who are better educated even raise healthier children. For the sake of Saudi Arabia's future, the government should give women the rights they deserve as human beings.

*Deputy Director for the Middle East and North Africa at Amnesty International: Amnesty International is probably the most influential global human rights group. This position makes him the second most important person in the Middle East and North Africa branch of the organization.

CUE TO DEBATE

Discuss the questions. Your answers will be a cue for your debate speech.

Do you think women with a foreign driver's license should drive in Saudi Arabia?

Do you think individual's choices governed by social rules always bring good results?

BUILD TO DEBATE

Study the essential vocabulary for this lesson to build knowledge for debate.

1 LANGUAGE TO COMPREHEND
Choose the correct synonym for each word or phrase.

1. **sinful** — a. helpful — b. dangerous — c. evil

2. **permission** — a. agreement — b. special paper — c. support

3. **modernize** — a. advance — b. collapse — c. worsen

4. **voices** — a. opinions — b. sounds — c. singers

5. **protests** — a. events to watch — b. events to complain — c. events to try

6. **status** — a. appearance — b. social position — c. nation

2 LANGUAGE TO DEBATE
Choose the correct definition of each word or phrase.

1. A lot of **religious leaders** in Saudi Arabia believe that it is sinful for women to drive.
   a. spiritual people
   b. careful people

2. After one woman was **arrested**, many other women decided to risk driving, too.
   a. given a video
   b. taken by the police

3. Arab women believe that the government should guarantee them their basic **human rights**.
   a. rights inherent to all human beings
   b. rights inherent to a minority group

THINK TO DEBATE

Think and share ideas to explore the debatable issues in the story. You may use the cues. You may need to change the form.

1. Why aren't women allowed to drive in Saudi Arabia?

• religious leaders • sinful

2. Other than not being allowed to drive, what else are women not allowed to do in Saudi Arabia?

• vote • permission

3. Why does Saudi Arabia want to make many changes in the country?

• modernize • comfortable

4. Do you think women are safer if they're not allowed to drive? Why or why not?

• accidents • other dangers

5. How do you think Manal al-Sharif and the other women felt about their decision to drive?

• proud • not regret

6. What might happen to women in Saudi Arabia if they choose to drive?

• be arrested • beat

7. When did women in Saudi Arabia first decide to drive, and what happened?

• punished • professors

8. How could Saudi society improve if women had more rights?

• children • healthier

The Road to Freedom 2A

LESSON 2
DEBATE CURRENT ISSUES

2B DEBATE CHAMPION

ARGUMENT TO DEBATE

Label each part of the arguments. Use "R" for reasons, "E" for evidence, "P" for pro arguments and "C" for con arguments. Then, place the reasons and evidence on the correct side of the debate.

> **Resolution:** Arab women should value social rules more than personal beliefs.

PRO OR CON	REASON OR EVIDENCE	ARGUMENT CHAMPION
		1. Following accepted social rules may cause others to suffer.
		2. Violating social rules can be dangerous.
		3. Many women have been arrested and members of one Facebook group have threatened to beat them.
		4. Since mothers don't fight for their human rights, the children of Saudi Arabia have less education and more health problems.
		5. Violating social rules can require one to disobey authority figures.
		6. Many men and women disagree with Saudi society because they think the rules do not keep women safe.
		7. Sometimes society does not have the best answer.
		8. Manal al-Sharif disobeyed religious leaders who said that it is sinful for a woman to drive.

TEAM A PRO

Arab women should value social rules more than personal beliefs because _____. (**A**ssertion) (**R**eason)
For example, _____. (**E**vidence)

REASON	EVIDENCE

TEAM B CON

Arab women should NOT value social rules more than personal beliefs because _____. (**A**ssertion) (**R**eason)
For example, _____. (**E**vidence)

REASON	EVIDENCE

RESEARCH TO DEBATE

Research the following questions to make your argument strong. You may use the cues.

1. What are some things that women in Saudi Arabia are not allowed to do? (Saudi Arabian women's rights)
2. How healthy and well-educated are Saudi Arabian children? (health standards in Saudi Arabia / international education rankings)
3. What problems do foreign women face when they visit Saudi Arabia? (foreign women in Saudi Arabia)

UNIT 1 LESSON 2 Debate Current Issues

FORMAT TO DEBATE
Read and learn what Public Forum Debate is.

Public Forum Debate

Public Forum Debate is another popular debate format. It is also sometimes called Ted Turner Debate and was used on CNN's Crossfire program. In Public Forum Debate, each team has two speakers, and each speaker gives two speeches. The first time they speak, each speaker gives a constructive speech and presents new reasons and evidence. The second time they focus on explaining these reasons more clearly.

After two speeches, one for each side, there is a crossfire round for the two speakers who just spoke to ask each other questions and answer them. After the summary speeches, all four debaters can ask questions. This is a good opportunity for the teams to show how their ideas are different. In Public Forum Debate, the debate topic is usually called the resolution. Unlike other debate formats, Public Forum Debate can start with either side for or against the topic. Debaters flip a coin to decide which team will start and what side that team will argue.

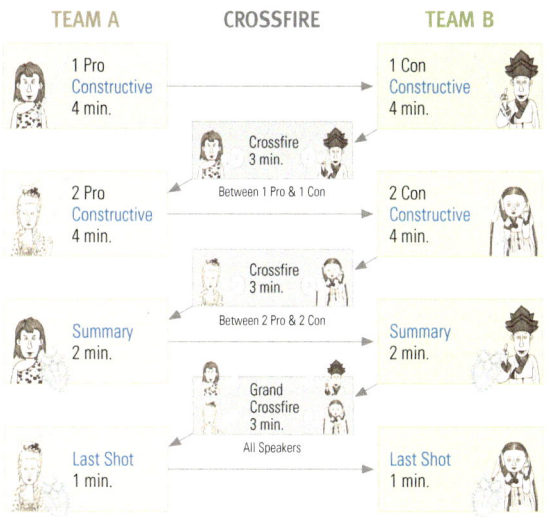

DEBATE KEYNOTES

In the debate format diagram, the characters who are holding loudspeakers share their ideas by asking and answering questions. In the Debate Champion series, assume that Team A always wins the coin toss and chooses to speak first. Team B chooses the con side.

APPLY TO DEBATE
Study the Public Forum Debate format chart above and fill in the blanks. Then draw arrows to show the order of the speeches.

TEAM A PRO	CROSSFIRE	TEAM B CON
First .... Constructive	⟶	First ....
	First Crossfire: .... and First Con	
Second Pro		.... Constructive
	.... : Second Pro and	
.... Summary Speech		
	.... : All speakers	
		The Last Shot

DEVELOP TO DEBATE

Insert the reasons and evidence from Argument to Debate into the chart in a logical order. Perform the debate in two groups. Instead of a coin toss, Pro team will begin.

Resolution: Arab women should value social rules more than personal beliefs.

First Pro Constructive Speech

DEFINITION This debate says that women in Saudi Arabia should *obey the rules of society* and avoid driving even if *they think this is wrong*. (obey, wrong)

TEAM LINE Arab women can live well and proud by following social rules.

REASON _____ (dangerous)

EVIDENCE _____

Second Pro Constructive Speech

TEAM LINE _____

REBUTTAL What the other team said is not always true. Social rules themselves rarely cause others to suffer. Disobeying social rules causes more problems.

REASON _____

EVIDENCE _____

Summary Speech

TEAM LINE _____

REBUTTAL What the other team said is not relevant. Social rules are designed to protect people and give them freedom.

DETAIL Many people believe that *social rules to keep women from driving* help to *keep women safe*. (social rules, keep ~ from, keep ~ safe)

The Last Shot

In Public Forum Debate, each team summarizes the strongest argument when giving the big picture in the last shot.

TEAM LINE _____

THE BIG PICTURE We agree that *Arab women should value social rules more than personal beliefs* because *valuing social rules keeps them safe. / valuing social rules allows them to follow their morals.* (safe OR follow, morals)

The first speakers speak in the first crossfire. The second speakers speak in the second crossfire. Pro team should always ask the first question.

First Crossfire

Second Crossfire

Grand Crossfire

DEBATE CHAMPION TIP

The Coin Toss and the Speaker Order

It is true that Public Forum Debate always begins with a coin toss, but at this language learning stage, it is easier and more accessible for the pro side to practice speaking first to avoid causing learners' confusion.

Debate Format

Public Forum Debate

TEAM B CON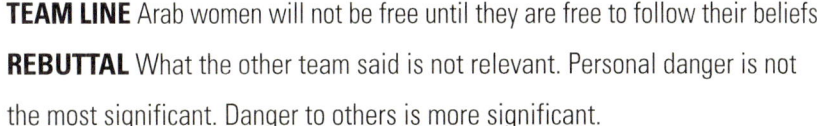

 ### First Con Constructive Speech

TEAM LINE Arab women will not be free until they are free to follow their beliefs.

REBUTTAL What the other team said is not relevant. Personal danger is not the most significant. Danger to others is more significant.

REASON

EVIDENCE

 ### Second Con Constructive Speech

TEAM LINE

REBUTTAL What the other team said is not always true. We can often follow personal beliefs without disobeying. There can be a better way.

REASON

EVIDENCE

 ### Summary Speech

TEAM LINE

REBUTTAL What the other team said is not significant. The benefits to women when they follow social rules are much smaller than the benefits when they follow their personal beliefs.

DETAIL The women who _____ (choose to drive, not regret)

 ### The Last Shot

TEAM LINE

THE BIG PICTURE We do not agree that _____

because _____ (cause pain OR not valuable)

CROSSFIRE TO DEBATE

Write the number of each question by the right speaker. You can also use your own ideas during the crossfire. Take turns to ask and answer completely and politely.

CROSSFIRE CHAMPION

1. Have any women actually been hurt for driving in Saudi Arabia?
2. Is disobeying authority figures really such a terrible thing?
3. Isn't it true that children are also hurt when their mothers are in danger?
4. How can you prove that one person has a better answer than the majority of society?

LINK TO DEBATE
Read the situation below. Then, use strong arguments to become a debate champion.

ALLISON'S DILEMMA

In class, Allison's history teacher wants the students to read a new book. The book looks very interesting, but Allison knows that her parents think the author of the book has views that are too narrow and inflexible. They would tell her that it is a bad influence on her, and it could encourage her to make bad choices. Allison's teacher says that the book is important to her understanding of history. The book doesn't seem to bother any of the other students, but Allison really feels uncomfortable. She wants to ask the teacher to let her choose another book, but it is a group project. If the teacher doesn't let her read another book, and Allison doesn't read it anyway, she will get a bad grade.

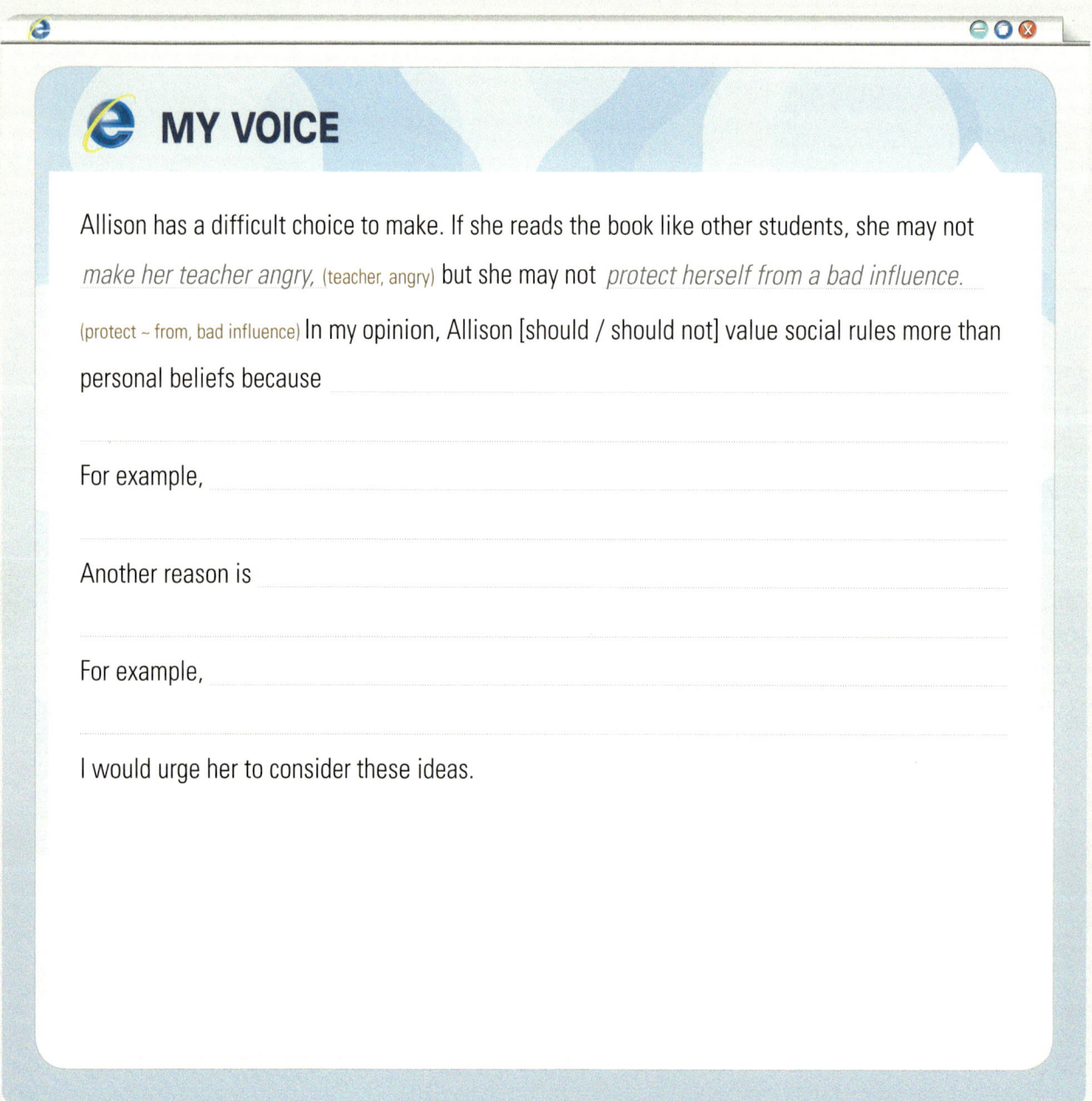

MY VOICE

Allison has a difficult choice to make. If she reads the book like other students, she may not *make her teacher angry,* (teacher, angry) but she may not *protect herself from a bad influence.* (protect ~ from, bad influence) In my opinion, Allison [should / should not] value social rules more than personal beliefs because _____

For example, _____

Another reason is _____

For example, _____

I would urge her to consider these ideas.

UNIT 2
We Need Help to Overcome Our Problems

The Secret Garden by Frances Hodgson Burnett
LITERATURE TO DEBATE

LISTEN TO DEBATE Track 3

Listen and number each box. Take notes while you listen and tell the story using the cues. You may need to change the form.

- amazed
- impress
- come back
- running

- rainy
- crying
- can't walk
- very selfish

- secret garden
- bury
- search and find
- beautiful

- selfish
- die
- uncle
- travel

| LESSON 3 | Debate Literature | The Secret Garden | Asian Parliamentary Debate |
| LESSON 4 | Debate Current Issues | Fighting for Peace | Public Forum Debate |

LESSON 3: DEBATE LITERATURE

3A SCHEMA CHAMPION

READ TO DEBATE Track 4

Read the story carefully, paying special attention to the thoughts and behaviors of the main characters.

FACT FILE		
	Context	The story takes places at the beginning of the 1900s. It starts in India, but most of the story happens in Northern England.
	Publication Date	The Secret Garden was written in England between 1906 and 1909 and published in 1909.
	Author	Frances Hodgson Burnett was an English-American playwright and writer. She lived from 1849 to 1924.
	Genre	Coming-of-age

The Secret Garden, by Frances Hodgson Burnett

When Mary Lennox was sent to Misselthwaite Manor to live with her uncle, everybody said she was the most **disagreeable-looking** child ever seen. It was true, too. She had been born in India and had often been sick. Her skin was yellowish, making her not at all pretty. She wasn't a very pleasant girl, either. She was selfish and never thought much of being kind, happy or even interested in anything. Mary's parents were English, but they ignored her. She had always been taken care of by an Indian servant.

When Mary was nine years old, everyone in her home grew very ill and died. Mary was left all alone, completely forgotten in her parents' home. As she had neither father nor mother, she was taken away and was soon sent back to England to live with her uncle, Archibald Craven.

Mr. Craven was an unhappy man with hunched* shoulders. His wife had died ten years earlier, and he had never **recovered** from the grief. He had closed most of the rooms in his large house and almost never stayed at home himself. He spent most of his time traveling and trying to be anywhere but at Misselthwaite Manor.

On Mary's first morning at Misselthwaite, Martha, a maid, sent her outside to play in the gardens. Just before Mary went outside, Martha added, "One of the gardens is locked up. No one has been in it for ten years. Mr. Craven had it shut when his wife died. He won't let anyone go inside. It was his wife's garden. He locked the

*hunched: bent forwards

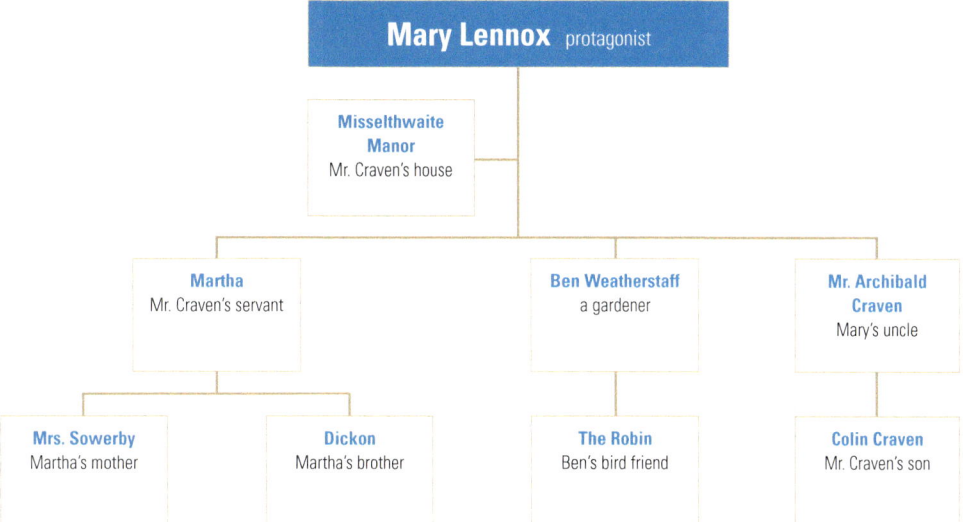

door, dug a hole and buried the key."

Mary was very curious about this garden. She wondered what it would look like and whether there were any flowers still alive in it. Mary did not find the locked garden that day, but she began to spend most of her days outside. She befriended an old gardener called Ben Weatherstaff. Ben told her about a robin who lived in the garden and kept him company. She began to talk to the robin and **counted** it as her friend.

One day, Mary asked Ben how to find the door to the secret garden. Ben suddenly started working and looked unfriendly, "There was a door ten years ago, but there isn't now," he said. "Don't be nosy and get into other people's business. I must get my work done. You go play. I don't have time."

Inside the house, Martha told Mary many stories about Martha's own family. She told her about her mother, Mrs. Sowerby, and about her brother, Dickon. She said that Dickon made friends with the plants and animals. The sheep knew him, and the birds ate out of his hands. Soon Mary became very interested in Dickon and Mrs. Sowerby. She asked Martha if she could meet them, and Martha said that someday she probably would.

Mary continued to look for the key to the garden, and one day, the little robin hopped over to a small hill of dirt. It looked like the dirt had been moved recently, and Mary began to move it away. Soon she found an old key. "Perhaps it has been buried for ten years," she said in a whisper. "Perhaps it is the key to the garden!"

After Mary had found the key, all she had to do was find the door to the garden. She began her search at once. The next day, the robin led her to a little door hidden behind some ivy. Mary moved the ivy aside and tried the key in the door. It fit perfectly. Mary opened the door, **slipped through** it and shut it behind her. She was standing inside the secret garden.

For the next several days, Mary looked for signs of life in the garden. She tried to learn everything she could about gardening, and she carefully tended* the flowers. She didn't tell anyone that she had found the garden, but she asked Martha for a favor. She asked her to write to Dickon and ask him to bring some gardening tools for her. Soon, Dickon came and gave her the tools. She decided she could trust Dickon and took him to the secret garden.

All this time, Mary had become quite a bit more agreeable. She began to grow stronger and healthier. The yellow left her face, and she was no longer an ugly child. She was even learning to be a little bit more polite to the people around her.

One day, it rained all day, and Mary couldn't go outside. She played in the house all day, and at night she couldn't sleep. She listened to the wind and the rain, and then she heard a sound that wasn't wind or rain. She heard crying and went to see where the sound came from. She walked down a dark hallway, and the sound seemed to be closer. She went through one door and then another, and then she saw a boy lying on a bed. The boy stared at her and asked, "Who are you? Are you a ghost?"

"No, I am not," Mary answered, half frightened. "Are you one?" As the two children talked, Mary learned that the boy's name was Colin Craven, and he was Mr. Craven's son.

Colin's eyes looked so much like his mother's eyes that his father couldn't look at him. The boy was weak, and most people thought that, if he lived to adulthood, he would be a **hunchback**. Even Colin thought that he would soon die, and that's why he had been crying. No one wanted to make Colin sicker, so everyone did exactly what he wanted. He was very spoiled.

Mary enjoyed talking to Colin. It was good to have a friend in the house, and as it rained all week, she talked to him every day. When the rain stopped, Mary went out to the garden and met Dickon. Colin was very angry. He **commanded** Mary to visit him, but she did not.

That night, Colin became very angry and **threw a fit**. He was so loud that Mary woke up on the other side of the house. She went to his room and shouted, "You stop! I hate you! Everybody hates you! You will scream yourself to death in a minute, and I wish you would!" No one had ever talked to Colin this way. He was shocked. "If you scream another scream," Mary said, "I'll scream, too. I can scream louder than you can, and I'll frighten you!" Colin stopped screaming. He also stopped demanding that Mary visit him.

Over the next few days, Mary explained to Colin that he was not really sick. He was just weak. She believed that Colin could become strong if he would just go outside and visit the secret garden. Mary and Colin made a plan to go

---

*tended: took care of (plants)

outside. They said they would visit the gardens and that they didn't want any adults around.

Mary took Colin to the secret garden. It was beautiful, and Colin was amazed. He had never seen anything like it before. After a while, Ben, the gardener, came into the garden. He was upset to see the children in the garden that was supposed to be locked. Then, he noticed Colin, and he became more shocked than angry. "You're the poor **cripple**," said Ben in surprise.

Now, Colin was angry. "I'm not a cripple!" he cried out furiously. "I'm not!" Colin sat straight up in his chair. Then, without thinking about it, he took the wrappings off of his legs and got out of his wheelchair. He stood up for the first time in his life.

From that day on, Colin went outside almost every day. Behind the walls of the secret garden, he practiced standing. Then, he practiced walking on his own, and soon he could run. Mary, Dickon and Ben spent many pleasant hours in the garden with Colin. Even Mrs. Sowerby came to the garden to see how Colin was improving. They didn't tell anyone in the house, though. They wanted Mr. Craven to be **genuinely** surprised when he saw Colin.

After a time, Mrs. Sowerby sent a letter to Mr. Craven. "Please, sir," it said, "I would come home if I were you. I think you would be glad to come, and I think your wife would ask you to come if she were here."

Mr. Craven read the letter twice and then planned his trip back to Misselthwaite. When he arrived at the house, he immediately went to the secret garden. As soon as Mr. Craven got to the garden and began to look for the key, the door to the garden opened and Colin Craven came running out. Mr. Craven had to hold his arms out to keep Colin from running into him.

Perhaps for the first time since the death of his wife, Mr. Craven smiled. He was deeply touched by seeing that his son could **overcome** his challenges and become a strong and lively boy, and he was delighted to find that the garden was still alive. Together, Mr. Craven and his son walked out of the garden.

From the house, the servants looked out the windows. "Look there," said one servant, "That's unusual. Look what's coming across the grass." Mr. Craven was walking across the grass, and many had never seen him so happy. By his side, with his head up and his eyes full of laughter, Colin walked as strongly as any ordinary boy.

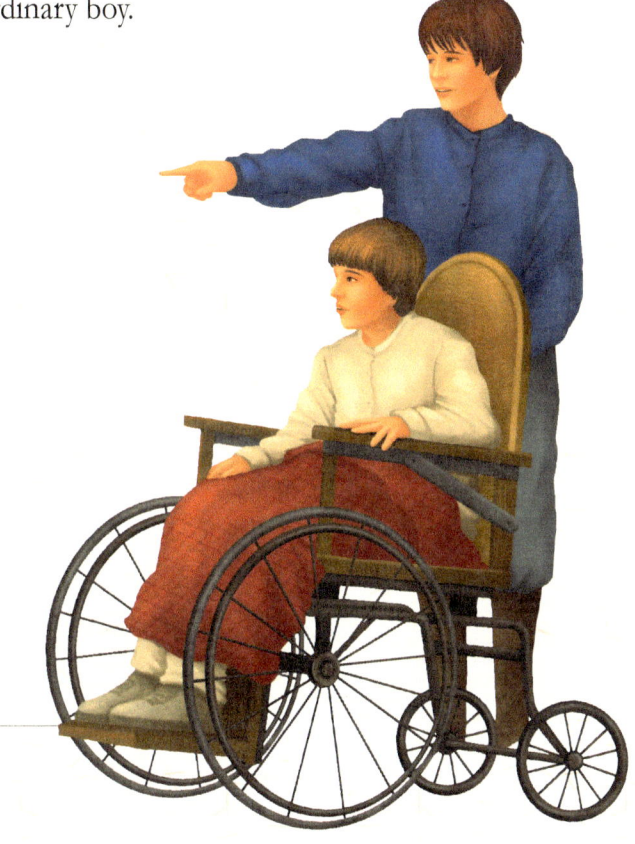

CUE TO DEBATE
Discuss the questions. Your answers will be a cue for your debate speech.

Do you think Colin could have learned to walk without Mary's help?

How do you think Mr. Craven recovered from the grief of his wife's death?

BUILD TO DEBATE
Study the essential vocabulary for this lesson to build knowledge for debate.

1 LANGUAGE TO COMPREHEND
Choose the correct synonym for each word or phrase.

1. **disagreeable-looking** — a. mean b. searching hard c. not pleasant or pretty

2. **counted** — a. made a calculation b. tried to make c. considered

3. **slipped through** — a. looked past b. entered carefully c. fell between

4. **commanded** — a. ordered b. pleaded c. begged

5. **threw a fit** — a. played a game b. showed anger c. cried sadly

6. **genuinely** — a. truly b. unusually c. hopefully

2 LANGUAGE TO DEBATE
Choose the correct definition of each word or phrase.

1. When Mr. Craven saw his son walk, he finally **recovered** from his grief.
   a. found again
   b. got better

2. Colin thought he would be a **hunchback** when he grew up.
   a. person with a bent back
   b. person with good guesses

3. Everyone believed that Colin was a **cripple** because he never left his room.
   a. person who is selfish
   b. person who can't walk

4. Colin showed Ben that he could **overcome** his problem by standing up for the first time in his life.
   a. overlook
   b. get over

34 UNIT 2 LESSON 3 Debate Literature

THINK TO DEBATE

Think and share ideas to explore the debatable issues in the story. You may use the cues. You may need to change the form.

1. How did Mary find the key to the secret garden?

• robin • dirt

2. How were Mary and Colin similar at the beginning of the story?

• selfish • unhappy

3. Why did Mary decide to take Dickon to the garden?

• trust • plants

4. Why did Mary want Colin to visit the secret garden?

• nature • enjoy one's life

5. At what moment did Colin start to overcome his problem?

• shout • stand up

6. How did Colin learn to run?

• practice • not give up

7. Why did Colin work so hard to learn to walk and run?

• father • proud

8. How did Mr. Craven recover from the grief of his wife's death?

• running • cheerful

LESSON 3
DEBATE LITERATURE

3B DEBATE CHAMPION

ARGUMENT TO DEBATE

Label each part of the arguments. Use "R" for reasons, "E" for evidence, "G" for government arguments and "O" for opposition arguments. Then, place the reasons and evidence on the correct side of the debate.

> **Debate Topic:** We need help to overcome our problems.

GOVERNMENT OR OPPOSITION	REASON OR EVIDENCE	ARGUMENT CHAMPION
		1. Without Mary's strong actions, Colin couldn't have overcome his challenges.
		2. Other people cannot solve problems completely for someone else.
		3. People can overcome anything by themselves if they have a strong will.
		4. Colin had to decide he was not a cripple or a hunchback and take off his wrappings himself to solve his own problem. No one else could do it for him.
		5. Other people's strong actions make it easier to overcome problems.
		6. Colin practiced walking on his own almost every day, and he didn't stop practicing until he was able to run.
		7. After Mr. Craven saw Colin walk, he was able to recover from the grief of his wife's death.
		8. Seeing others inspires people to overcome their problems.

GOVERNMENT

We need help to overcome our problems because _____. For example, _____.
(**A**ssertion)   (**R**eason)   (**E**vidence)

REASON	EVIDENCE

OPPOSITION

We do NOT need help to overcome our problems because _____. For example, _____.
(**A**ssertion)   (**R**eason)   (**E**vidence)

REASON	EVIDENCE

FORMAT TO DEBATE
Read and learn what a definition is in a debate.

Definitions

The first part of any debate is the definition. This is where the first speaker explains what the debate will be about. In Asian Parliamentary Debate, this is always in the first affirmative speech, which is given by the Prime Minister.

In a debate, debaters can understand the same debate topic in different ways. By defining the debate topic clearly, debaters on both teams can avoid misunderstandings. Then, everyone can easily debate about the same thing, and the debate will be much clearer. The Prime Minister should choose a definition that is obvious and easy to understand. A definition should make sure that the debate topic is debatable so that both sides' arguments work. It is also important that the definition should not make the debate too difficult. Then, both teams can make good arguments for their side of the debate.

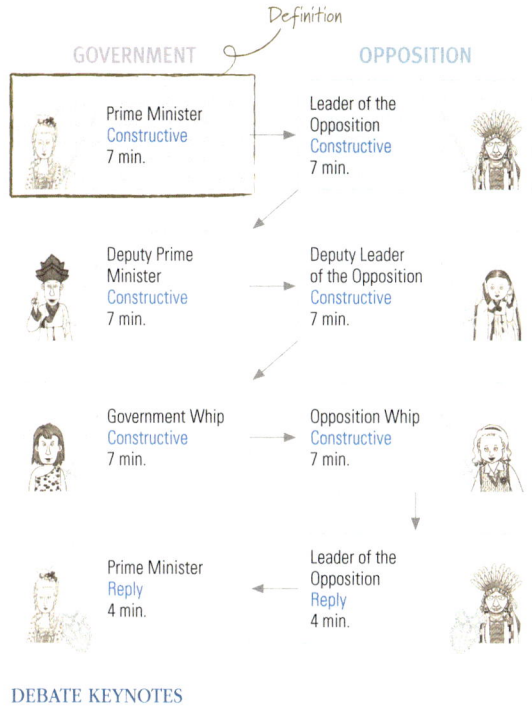

DEBATE KEYNOTES
The first speaker may make the definition very obvious by saying "this debate is about," "this debate argues that..." or "this debate says that...."

APPLY TO DEBATE
Read each debate topic and choose the best definition. Then, write the definition for #3 using the cues given.

DEBATE TOPIC	PRIME MINISTER'S DEFINITION
1. We need help to overcome our problems.	☐ a. People change more fully and become better if they have help from others. ☐ b. People should help others if they want to get over their problems.
2. We must help those who are weaker than us.	☐ a. Helping others is part of human nature. ☐ b. People have a responsibility to give up what they want to help someone who needs help.
3. We should ask others to help us in hard times.	 (problems with money or health, ask for)

The Secret Garden, by Frances Hodgson Burnett

DEVELOP TO DEBATE

Insert the reasons and evidence from Argument to Debate into the chart in a logical order. Perform the debate in two groups.

Debate Topic: This house believes that **we need help to overcome our problems.**

GOVERNMENT

Prime Minister's Constructive [First Affirmative Speech]

DEFINITION This debate argues that people change *more fully and become better* if they have *help from others.* (fully, better, from others)

TEAM LINE When we work together, we all do better than any of us could do alone.

REASON _____ (strong actions, easier)

EVIDENCE _____

Deputy Prime Minister's Constructive [Second Affirmative Speech]

TEAM LINE _____

REBUTTAL What the other team said is not always true. Even though people don't solve problems for us, they make it possible for us to do better. They can help us through their own behavior.

REASON _____

EVIDENCE _____

Government Whip's Constructive [Third Affirmative Speech]

TEAM LINE _____

REBUTTAL What the other team said is not always true. Some things are simply too difficult to accomplish only with one's strong will.

DETAIL Mary could not have *found the key without the bird's help* because *digging up everything around the garden would be too hard.* (without the bird's help, digging up, too hard)

Prime Minister's Reply [Affirmative Reply Speech]

TEAM LINE _____

REBUTTAL What the other team said is not true. It takes much more than independence to grow strong.

THE BIG PICTURE We believe that _____

because together we can _____

_____ (be inspired, more easily)

Debate Format

Asian Parliamentary Debate

OPPOSITION

Leader of the Opposition's Constructive [First Negative Speech]

TEAM LINE Independence is the key to strong growth.

REBUTTAL What the other team said is not relevant. Even if other people's strong actions make it easier, it may not be enough to solve the problem.

REASON _____ (solve problems)

EVIDENCE

Deputy Leader of the Opposition's Constructive [Second Negative Speech]

TEAM LINE

REBUTTAL What the other team said is not significant. People can just as easily get inspiration from within themselves.

REASON

EVIDENCE

Opposition Whip's Constructive [Third Negative Speech]

TEAM LINE

REBUTTAL What the other team said is not always true. Sometimes, people can easily solve their problems using curiosity, not others' help.

DETAIL Out of curiosity, Mary was able to start tending the garden, which helped her to change, before she _____ (have any help, from others)

Leader of the Opposition's Reply [Negative Reply Speech]

TEAM LINE

REBUTTAL What the other team said is not relevant. We all have the strength and independence necessary to overcome our problems well.

THE BIG PICTURE We do not believe that _____

because we are the ones who _____ (have the power, change oneself)

DEBATE CHAMPION TIP

The Jobs of Two Teams
Remember that, in a debate, the government's job is to show that the debate topic is true. The opposition has to show that the topic is not true. The opposition does not have to show that the opposite of the topic is true.

LESSON 4: DEBATE CURRENT ISSUES

4A SCHEMA CHAMPION

CRITIQUE TO DEBATE • Free MP3 File Downloadable @www.LARRABEE.co.kr

Read the story carefully, paying special attention to the motives and behaviors of the people involved in the issue.

Fighting for Peace

On a mountainous island between Indonesia and Australia lies the nation of Timor-Leste. It is small and very poor. It is also one of the world's newest countries, as it just gained independence in 1999. Since that time, the country has struggled in many ways, but it is working to overcome its problems.

In the 1500s, Portuguese traders started to trade spices and other items in Timor-Leste, and in 1642, the Portuguese **took control of** the island. The Portuguese controlled the area until 1974. When they left, there was no clear leader. Two political groups fought a very short **civil war**, and many people were killed or forced to leave their homes.

In 1976, Indonesia, the nation's closest neighbor, sent its army into the country. The Indonesian government said that this action was necessary to keep Timor-Leste peaceful. However, Indonesia treated the people of Timor-Leste cruelly, and the people were eager to be independent. In 1999, after some political problems in Indonesia, Indonesia gave Timor-Leste its independence.

From that time, Timor-Leste began the process of nation building. It would not be easy to build a peaceful and stable nation. The country needed to create ways to make its people able to live happy lives. The lack of money, electricity and other basic necessities made the people very **dissatisfied**. Additionally, there were many conflicts about who owned what land, and they were difficult to **resolve**. In short, the new government faced a lot of problems.

In 2006, almost one third of the army wrote a letter to the president to complain about

*mobs: a group of people involved in violent attacks

their problems. However, the government ignored the soldiers, and in April, the dissatisfied soldiers began to fight. Suddenly, the whole country was fighting, and many people had to leave their homes for safety. Mobs* and gangs killed people and destroyed **property** in the capital city.

The government of Timor-Leste had lost control, and they asked for help from Australia, Malaysia, New Zealand and Portugal. These countries sent people from their armies to Timor-Leste. Soon, the violence began to slow, and the country became more peaceful.

In August of 2006, the United Nations also decided to help Timor-Leste. The UN sent 1,500 police officers to help **maintain** peace in the country. These foreign police officers helped the local police officers and inspired them to do their best for their country.

The UN **peacekeeping mission** appeared to be successful, but the Secretary-General of the UN said that it was important for Timor-Leste to take responsibility. He said that the UN could not make Timor-Leste into a strong nation. The government of Timor-Leste would have to work hard to achieve this goal. It would take a lot of effort to make people respect the rule of law so that the country could be successful.

Then, in 2008, a group of men attacked the president. He was badly injured but soon recovered. In the meantime, the government of Timor-Leste did everything it could to **restore** peace. For a few weeks, the government didn't let people meet in large groups and required people to stay in their homes at night. The police worked hard to find and arrest anyone who might be causing a problem.

Worldwide, people were impressed with the government's **response** to the crisis. The government used the laws of the country to maintain peace. The people stayed calm because the government encouraged them to believe that it could solve the problem.

Since that time, Timor-Leste has been an increasingly peaceful country. The government is taking control, and people are beginning to believe that the country will be strong. As the government solves more and more of the people's problems, Timor-Leste will become a stable and peaceful nation.

CUE TO DEBATE

Discuss the questions. Your answers will be a cue for your debate speech.

Do you think Timor-Leste would be peaceful now if the UN and other countries had not helped them in 2006? Why or why not?

What else do you think the president of Timor-Leste could do to make the country peaceful?

BUILD TO DEBATE

Study the essential vocabulary for this lesson to build knowledge for debate.

1 LANGUAGE TO COMPREHEND
Choose the correct synonym for each word or phrase.

1. **took control of** — a. invaded — b. moved — c. visited
2. **civil war** — a. war with many countries — b. war between neighbors — c. war in one country
3. **dissatisfied** — a. discontented — b. insulting — c. pleased
4. **resolve** — a. fight over — b. settle — c. try again
5. **property** — a. goods — b. huge land — c. something owned
6. **response** — a. message — b. reaction — c. feedback

2 LANGUAGE TO DEBATE
Choose the correct definition of each word or phrase.

1. Timor-Leste can become a stable country if it can **maintain** peace.
   a. keep
   b. fix

2. The UN **peacekeeping mission** to Timor-Leste helped the country to become more stable.
   a. effort to stop fighting
   b. search for peace

3. The government of Timor-Leste worked hard to handle the crisis and **restore** peace.
   a. give back
   b. reestablish

42 UNIT 2 LESSON 4 Debate Current Issues

THINK TO DEBATE

Think and share ideas to explore the debatable issues in the story. You may use the cues. You may need to change the form.

1 Why were there many conflicts in Timor-Leste after 1999?

• necessities • conflicts

2 Why did the government of Timor-Leste ask other countries to help its nation in 2006?

• control • peaceful

3 What did the UN do to help Timor-Leste in 2006?

• maintain • peacekeeping

4 What did the UN Secretary-General say that Timor-Leste had to do? Do you think he was right?

• responsibility • rule of law

5 What did Timor-Leste do to restore peace in 2008? Was this a good idea?

• extra rules • keep ~ safe

6 How did other countries feel about the Timor-Leste government's response to the crisis in 2008? Why?

• impressed • by oneself

7 Do you think that the UN should help Timor-Leste again? Why or why not?

• stable • new country

8 Imagine you are a citizen of Timor-Leste. Do you believe Timor-Leste can solve another crisis like the ones in 2006 and 2008 on its own?

• continue to improve • too serious

LESSON 4
DEBATE CURRENT ISSUES

4B DEBATE CHAMPION

ARGUMENT TO DEBATE

Label each part of the arguments. Use "R" for reasons, "E" for evidence, "P" for pro arguments and "C" for con arguments. Then, place the reasons and evidence on the correct side of the debate.

Resolution: Countries need help to overcome their problems.

PRO OR CON	REASON OR EVIDENCE	ARGUMENT CHAMPION
		1. Others' strong actions make it easier to overcome problems.
		2. Because the UN sent 1,500 police officers in a peacekeeping mission, it was easier for Timor-Leste to overcome its problems.
		3. The police force of Timor-Leste was inspired by the international police officers, and they worked harder to maintain peace.
		4. The UN Secretary-General said that the UN could not make Timor-Leste into a strong nation. Timor-Leste had to take responsibility for nation building.
		5. Other countries cannot solve problems completely for another country.
		6. After the 2008 crisis, Timor-Leste worked hard to make people respect the laws of the country to solve the problem and finally restored peace by itself.
		7. Seeing others inspires people to overcome their problems.
		8. Countries can overcome anything by themselves if they have a strong will.

TEAM A PRO

Countries need help to overcome their problems because _____ (Reason). For example, _____ (Evidence).

REASON	EVIDENCE

TEAM B CON

Countries do NOT need help to overcome their problems because _____ (Reason). For example, _____ (Evidence).

REASON	EVIDENCE

RESEARCH TO DEBATE

Research the following questions to make your argument strong. You may use the cues.

1. What is the UN's role in Timor-Leste now? What did the UN do there most recently? (UN activity Timor-Leste)
2. Are the people of Timor-Leste satisfied with their country? (Timor-Leste citizen challenges)
3. What is the government of Timor-Leste doing for its people? (Timor-Leste government development)

FORMAT TO DEBATE
Read and learn what team lines are.

Team Lines

One of the most important parts of every debate speech is the team line. Every speaker on a debate team should give the team line. The team line is a kind of main idea or thesis statement for the team. Each team should focus their arguments around one big idea and state this idea in a simple way. Then, debaters should repeat the team line at the beginning of their turn.

Team lines have a unique purpose in a debate. One team gives the definition to define the debate for both teams. However, each team gives its own team line to explain its own main idea clearly. The team line says what the team believes and why. The purpose of giving a team line is to help the audience and judges remember what the team wants to say by repeating it consistently, and this memorable expression helps makes the team's arguments clearer.

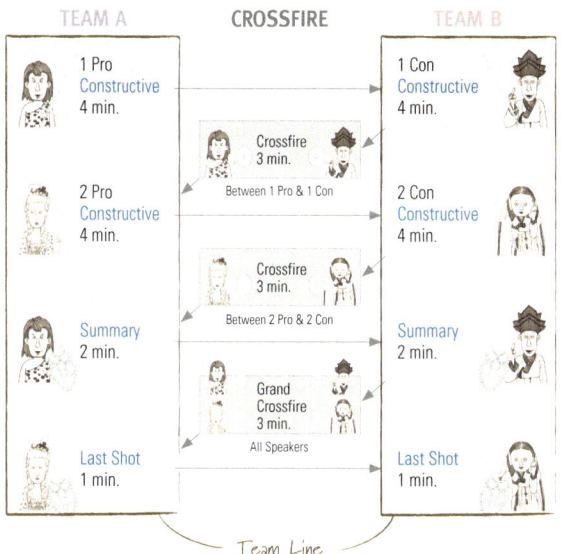

DEBATE KEYNOTES

The act of debating is beneficial in that debaters can learn the importance of teamwork. The team line shows that debating is a team event in which the two speakers on each team work together as a team.

APPLY TO DEBATE
Read the resolutions and team lines below. Then, mark whether each team line is for the pro or con team.

RESOLUTION	Countries need help to overcome their problems.	PRO	CON
TEAM LINE	a. To grow strong, countries must learn to solve problems on their own.	☐	☐
	b. Successful countries grow strong through help.	☐	☐

RESOLUTION	Stronger countries should help weaker countries.	PRO	CON
TEAM LINE	a. Being a good neighbor means helping the weak to become strong.	☐	☐
	b. The weak become strong by facing their challenges.	☐	☐

RESOLUTION	Countries must ask for help when they face problems.	PRO	CON
TEAM LINE	a. The brave only ask for help when there is no other choice.	☐	☐
	b. Responsible countries are happy to let others help.	☐	☐

DEVELOP TO DEBATE

Insert the reasons and evidence from Argument to Debate into the chart in a logical order. Perform the debate in two groups. Instead of a coin toss, Pro team will begin.

> Resolution:
> **Countries need help to overcome their problems.**

TEAM A *PRO* CROSSFIRE

First Pro Constructive Speech
DEFINITION This debate says that countries overcome *their problems with fewer challenges* if they have *help from other countries.*

TEAM LINE Successful countries grow strong through help.

REASON _____ (easier)

EVIDENCE _____

First Crossfire

Second Pro Constructive Speech
TEAM LINE _____

REBUTTAL What the other team said is not relevant. Countries use the help of other countries just to help them start solving their problems.

REASON _____

EVIDENCE _____

Second Crossfire

Summary Speech
TEAM LINE _____

REBUTTAL What the other team said is not always true. Some problems cannot be solved with just a strong will.

DETAIL The government of Timor-Leste knew it _____ in 2006. *(need help, ask ~ to help)*
_____

Grand Crossfire

The Last Shot
TEAM LINE _____

THE BIG PICTURE We agree that _____
_____

because they can _____
_____ *(be inspired OR overcome ~ more easily)*

DEBATE CHAMPION TIP

Reasons in Speeches
A constructive speech in a debate is a speech that gives new reasons. Other speeches can give new evidence and explain the reasons that were already given. Any speech can explain a reason or rebut a reason from the other side.

Debate Format

Public Forum Debate

TEAM B CON

First Con Constructive Speech

TEAM LINE To grow strong, countries must learn to solve their own problems.

REBUTTAL What the other team said is not relevant. Even if others' strong actions make it easier, it may not be enough to solve the problem.

REASON

EVIDENCE

Second Con Constructive Speech

TEAM LINE

REBUTTAL What the other team said is not significant. Inspiration from seeing others does not help much. Countries need to look inside themselves.

REASON

EVIDENCE

Summary Speech

TEAM LINE

REBUTTAL What the other team said is not always true. Every country has the resources and potential it needs to solve its problems if it really wants to.

DETAIL The government of Timor-Leste has shown that it has the

(ability, to maintain peace)

The Last Shot

TEAM LINE

THE BIG PICTURE We do not agree that

because they

(the only ones OR strong will)

CROSSFIRE TO DEBATE

Write the number of each question by the right speaker. You can also use your own ideas during the crossfire. Take turns to ask and answer completely and politely.

CROSSFIRE CHAMPION

1. How can you show that the police officers worked harder because they were inspired by other police officers?

2. Do you believe that the UN Secretary-General thought Timor-Leste had to solve their own problems even though the UN sent police officers to Timor-Leste?

3. Do you think countries can overcome anything even if they don't have all the resources and potential to make their strong will effective?

4. What exactly did the 1,500 police officers do to make it easier for Timor-Leste to overcome their problems?

Fighting for Peace 4B

LINK TO DEBATE

Read the situation below. Then, use strong arguments to become a debate champion.

PRESIDENT JONES' DILEMMA

President Jones is the president of a small island country in the Pacific Ocean. He is a good president, but his country is poor. Many of the citizens are dissatisfied with the government. They don't think the government does enough to help them. Now, many of the people are fighting in the streets. Some people even have to leave their homes to stay safe. President Jones wants his country to be peaceful again, but many of his police officers are afraid to go out into the streets. President Jones doesn't know if he can overcome this problem without help from other countries. He wonders if he should write a letter to the UN and his closest neighbors or if he should try to motivate people to solve the problem by themselves.

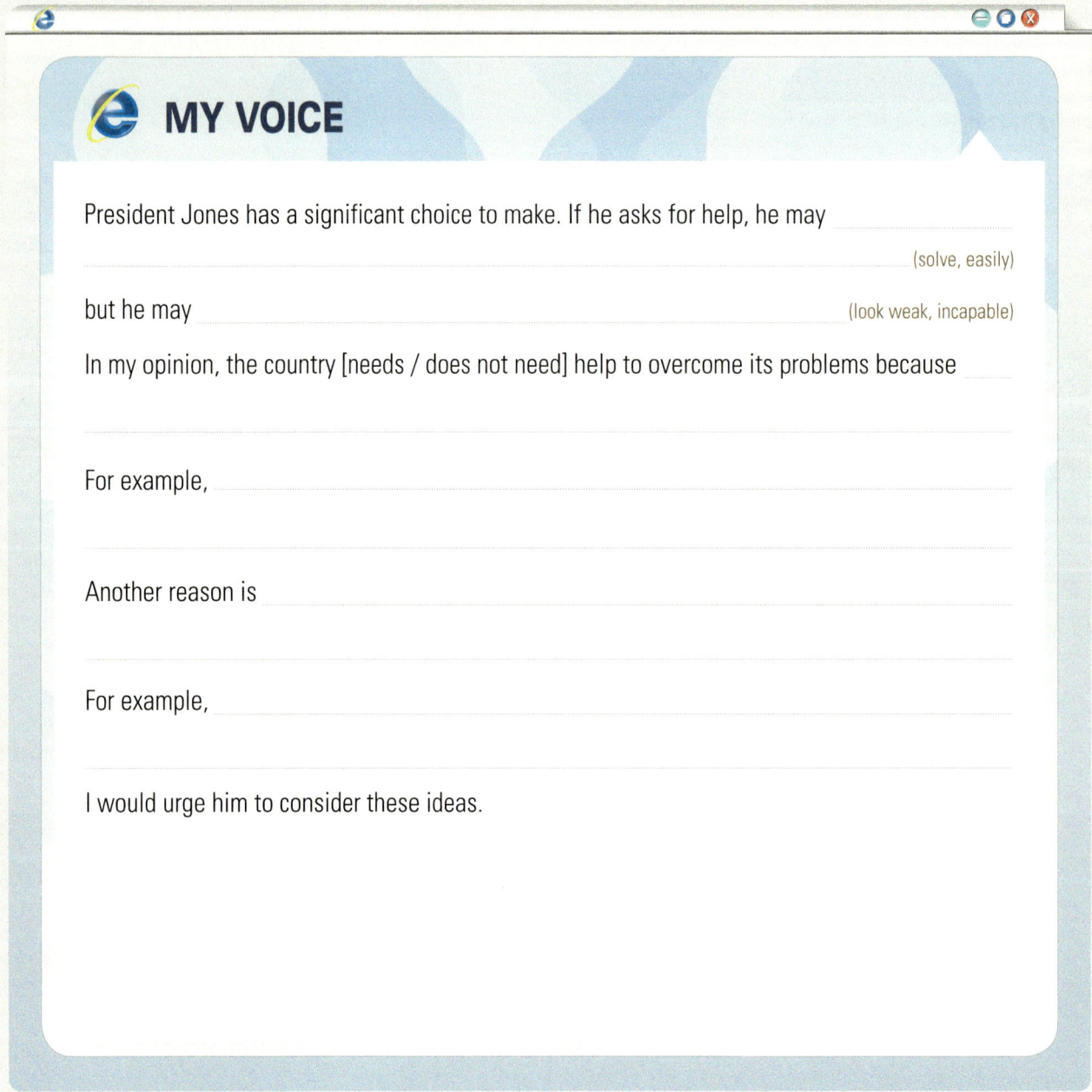

MY VOICE

President Jones has a significant choice to make. If he asks for help, he may _____
_____ (solve, easily)

but he may _____ (look weak, incapable)

In my opinion, the country [needs / does not need] help to overcome its problems because _____
_____

For example, _____
_____

Another reason is _____
_____

For example, _____
_____

I would urge him to consider these ideas.

UNIT 3
Good Rulers Have to Experience Ordinary People's Hardship

The Prince and the Pauper by Mark Twain
LITERATURE TO DEBATE

LISTEN TO DEBATE Track 5

Listen and number each box. Take notes while you listen and tell the story using the cues. You may need to change the form.

- thief
- king of England
- trade clothes
- similar

- run away
- upset
- stay away from
- trouble

- crown the new king
- believe
- agree
- be good to

- Tom Canty
- Prince Edward
- act more like
- please the king

LESSON 5 Debate Literature — The Prince and the Pauper — Asian Parliamentary Debate
LESSON 6 Debate Current Issues — Beyond Native Teachers — Public Forum Debate

LESSON 5: DEBATE LITERATURE

5A SCHEMA CHAMPION

READ TO DEBATE Track 6

Read the story carefully, paying special attention to the thoughts and behaviors of the main characters.

FACT FILE		
	Context	This story happens in and around London in January and February of 1547. This is the year that King Henry VIII died, and Edward VI became the king of England.
	Publication Date	The book was written in Connecticut around 1880 and was first published in Canada in 1881.
	Author	Mark Twain was born as Samuel Clemens. He was one of the greatest American humor writers of the 1800s. He lived from 1835 to 1910.
	Genre	Realistic Historical Fiction

The Prince and the Pauper, by Mark Twain

In the ancient city of London, on October 12, 1537, a boy was born to a poor family named Canty, who did not want him. On the same day another English child was born to a rich family named Tudor, who did want him. All England wanted him too, and everyone rejoiced when they heard of his birth.

The first boy was Tom Canty. His family lived in Offal Court, the poorest area in London. His father, John Canty, was a beggar and a thief, and he raised his son to be a beggar, even if he wasn't a thief. Tom's father made him beg every day and beat him **mercilessly** if he didn't gain enough money. Tom's grandmother also beat poor Tom regularly. However, his mother and his two sisters, Nan and Bet, were kind.

The second boy was Edward Tudor. His family lived in Westminster Palace just outside of London, the finest area in England. His father, Henry Tudor, was the great King Henry VIII, and he raised his son to be a king. Edward's father made him study every day and trained him for his **royal** responsibilities. Edward also passed many enjoyable hours with his sister, Lady Elizabeth, and with his cousin, Lady Jane Grey.

Tom Canty dreamed of being a better man. He even dreamed of seeing a prince. Father Andrew who lived near him, taught him to read and write and even taught him some Latin.

One day, when Tom was nine years old, he wandered* west. He walked right out of the city of London and up to the gates of Westminster. At the gates, a soldier threw Tom back into the street, but Edward Tudor had seen the act.

*wandered: walked without a plan to go anywhere specific

CHARACTER WEB

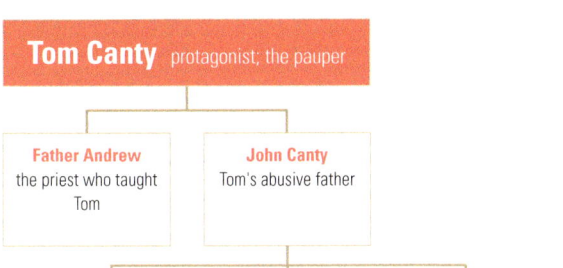
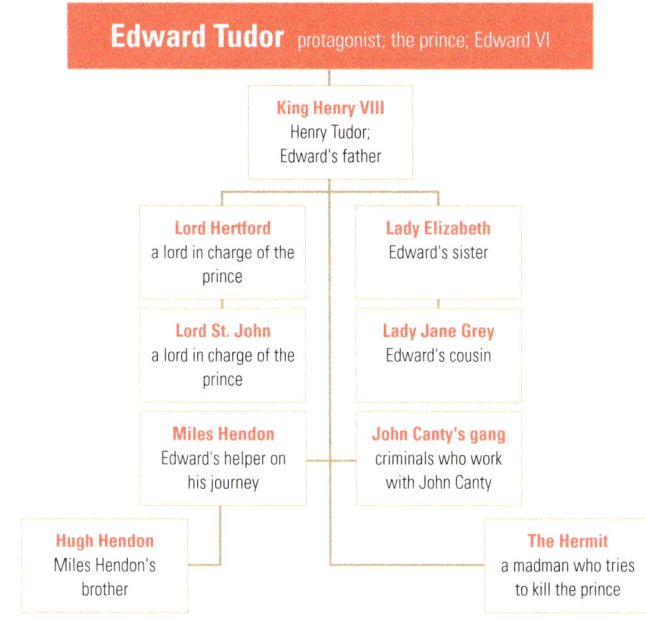

Prince Edward walked up to the soldier and commanded him to let the boy in. Seeing that Tom was hungry, the prince invited him into his royal rooms and commanded his servants to bring a fine meal. Tom was amazed by the palace, as he had never before seen any place that was not dirty, crowded and miserable. On the other hand, the prince could hardly believe Tom's tales of these dirty, crowded and miserable places. He could not imagine a place where beatings were common and food was not. He imagined that Tom had a life of complete freedom.

The prince listened carefully to everything that Tom said. Then he cried, "Oh, please, say no more. It's glorious! If I could wear clothes like yours and run barefoot in the mud just once, without anyone telling me not to, I think I would not want the crown!"

"And if I could wear your clothes, just once," started Tom.

The prince thought it was a wonderful idea. The two boys switched clothes and looked into the mirror, but there did not seem to have been any change! Except for their clothes, the two boys looked exactly alike. The prince noticed a **bruise** that Tom had received from the soldier. He left the room and went to punish the soldier, but when the soldier saw him, he didn't know the boy was the prince. He thought the boy was Tom Canty and threw him out into the street.

The prince told everyone that he was the prince, but everyone laughed at him, thinking he was mad. Finally, John Canty, took the prince by the collar and dragged him to his own home.

Tom Canty, back in the palace, became worried when the prince didn't return. He didn't want to stay in the palace. After a while, Lady Jane Grey came to talk to him, but she couldn't understand why he didn't know her. She thought the prince was mad and told others the news.

Henry VIII was very sad to think that his son was mad. He ordered that no one speak of it. He also ordered the boy to stop saying he was a poor boy from Offal Court. From then on, Lord St. John and Lord Hertford stayed with the boy and helped him whenever his mind failed.

Tom tried very hard to **adapt to** life at the court. He made many mistakes in trying to eat as a prince would eat. The two lords corrected Tom carefully, and slowly he learned the right way to behave. After Tom found a book on etiquette, his studies on how to behave at court began in earnest. Tom's etiquette improved quickly, and he was soon sent to a fine dinner in London.

Meanwhile, the prince had escaped from John Canty and was trying to get into the fine dinner. He became more upset when the people laughed at him and even tried to beat him. Then, as if out of nowhere, Miles Hendon appeared and told everyone to stop bothering the boy. Hendon didn't believe that the boy was the king, but he also didn't want him to be hurt.

Just then, a messenger said that Henry VIII had died. Tom Canty was told he was king. The true king, Edward, felt only sadness because the **tyrant** who had been a terror to others had always been gentle with him. He cried quietly.

Hendon promised to help the prince and took him to his home. He let the prince sleep in his bed while Hendon laid on the floor by the door. The prince didn't recognize how much kindness Hendon showed him, but he was still grateful. He granted Hendon the right to sit in the presence of the king and made him a knight.

The next morning, while Hendon was out, a man came and took the naive* prince to John Canty. When Hendon realized that the prince was gone, he tried to find him. However, John Canty had cleverly avoided him, and Hendon knew it would not be easy to find the boy.

At the palace, Tom went into the throne room to spend his first day as king. He thought that most of what kings had to do was really boring. Later, Tom saw a few prisoners being taken away to be killed. He asked what they had done and what proof had been shown against them. After hearing the answers, Tom didn't believe that the prisoners had committed any crimes at all. He ordered that they be set free.

John Canty had joined a gang in the countryside, and the prince had to join the criminals. When the prince told some people that the gang was stealing from them, the prince was able to run away. He ran to the house of a **hermit**. The hermit welcomed the prince and gave him food, but when he heard that he was Henry VIII's son, he became very angry. He tied the prince with rope and prepared to attack him with a knife.

Just then, Miles Hendon appeared searching for the prince. The hermit had to lead Miles Hendon off, thus sparing the prince's life. While the hermit and Miles Hendon were gone, John Canty and his friends came and took the

---

*naive: unaware of the real world; childish

prince. When the prince still refused to beg or steal, one of the members of the gang accused him of stealing and had him sent to prison.

The prince was about to be arrested and sentenced when Miles Hendon came. He begged the court to be kind to the boy, and Hendon and the prince got out of the town quietly. Hendon remembered his father's home at Hendon Hall. He had last visited the hall ten years earlier and decided to take the young prince there.

At Hendon Hall, Hendon found that his father was dead, and his brother was living there. His brother ruled the area through threats. Hendon's brother denied that he knew Hendon and even had him arrested and punished. When the prince protested, the officials decided to **whip** the prince for his bad behavior, but Hendon took the beating instead. For this, the prince gave him the title of Earl of Kent.

After Hendon was released, he and the prince headed back to London. It was almost the day for the new king to be crowned.

Before the coronation*, Tom Canty was paraded through the streets. Near his home, he saw his mother and was upset. The coronation began at Westminster Cathedral. Just before the crown could be placed on Tom Canty's head, the true prince walked up the aisle and said, "I **forbid** you to set the crown of England upon that head. I am the king!"

Everyone was amazed, but Tom Canty said, "Do not touch him. He is the king!" Everyone was forced to listen. They asked many questions to determine whether or not the prince was the king, but still, no one could decide for sure.

Someone asked, "Where is the Great Seal? Only the boy who was the prince can answer this question!" The prince was not certain. He could not remember exactly where he had put it. Then, Tom remembered that he had seen it. He helped the prince remember exactly what had happened on the day that they switched clothes.

Lord St. John ran to the palace to check on the location of the seal. Soon he came back with the seal in his hands. The royal robes* were taken off of Tom Canty's back and placed on Edward. The crown was placed on Edward's head, and he became Edward VI of England.

Edward VI was kind to his people. He rewarded Miles Hendon well and made Tom Canty the "King's Ward." He punished those who did evil during his time in the country, and he rewarded those who did good. From that day on, he was always just. If anyone doubted the wisdom of his kindness and mercy, the king would look at him and ask, "What do you know of **suffering** and **oppression**? I and my people know, but not you."

---

*coronation: a ceremony to crown a new king
*royal robes: long loose clothes worn by a king

CUE TO DEBATE
Discuss the questions. Your answers will be a cue for your debate speech.

Why do you think Edward VI was a kinder king than his father, Henry VIII?

Do you think Edward VI's education or experience was more important to him as king?

BUILD TO DEBATE
Study the essential vocabulary for this lesson to build knowledge for debate.

1 LANGUAGE TO COMPREHEND
Choose the correct synonym for each word or phrase.

1. **mercilessly** — a. quickly — b. carelessly — c. without any kindness
2. **royal** — a. of a king or emperor — b. grand — c. humble
3. **bruise** — a. small paper — b. skin injury — c. dirty spot
4. **adapt to** — a. change — b. get used to — c. care about
5. **hermit** — a. person who lives away from people — b. person who is strong — c. person who lives in a kingdom
6. **forbid** — a. permit — b. command — c. prohibit

2 LANGUAGE TO DEBATE
Choose the correct definition of each word or phrase.

1. Most people didn't like King Henry VIII because he was a **tyrant**.
   a. cruel ruler
   b. sage king

2. The officials decided to **whip** Hendon instead of Edward.
   a. worship
   b. beat

3. Edward experienced a lot of **suffering** while he was not at the palace.
   a. adventure
   b. pain and sorrow

4. The people of England didn't experience as much **oppression** under King Edward VI.
   a. unfair treatment from a strong ruler
   b. economic depression

THINK TO DEBATE

Think and share ideas to explore the debatable issues in the story. You may use the cues. You may need to change the form.

1 Why do you think Henry VIII encouraged his son to study every day?

• education • good ruler

2 Why do you think Tom didn't believe that the prisoners had done anything wrong?

• proof • punished unfairly

3 What do you think the prince learned when he experienced kindness from Hendon?

• sacrifice • good ruler

4 What do you think Tom and the prince learned from their experience of changing clothes?

• advantages • disadvantages

5 Do you think the laws that Edward VI made were really helpful to improve the lives of ordinary people? Why or why not?

• understand • people's need

6 Do you think that Edward's education helped him to make good laws for the people? Why or why not?

• suffering • how to think and communicate

7 Why were Lord Hertford and Lord St. John always near the prince and with him after he became king?

• advice • share knowledge

8 Do you think Edward would have been a kind king if he had not experienced the people's hardship? Why or why not?

• kind heart • learn from experience

LESSON 5
DEBATE LITERATURE

5B DEBATE CHAMPION

ARGUMENT TO DEBATE

Label each part of the arguments. Use "R" for reasons, "E" for evidence, "G" for government arguments and "O" for opposition arguments. Then, place the reasons and evidence on the correct side of the debate.

Debate Topic: Good rulers have to experience ordinary people's hardship.

GOVERNMENT OR OPPOSITION	REASON OR EVIDENCE	ARGUMENT CHAMPION
		1. After Edward became king, he was able to create fairer laws and not to be a tyrant because he knew which laws oppressed the people and had seen people being whipped and punished.
		2. King Henry encouraged his son to study every day to be a good ruler.
		3. As their advisors, Lord Hertford and Lord St. John helped Tom and Prince Edward to make good decisions.
		4. With a good education, a ruler has all of the knowledge necessary to be a good ruler.
		5. By experiencing people's hardship, rulers gain the ability to create practical solutions.
		6. Rulers cannot study and learn enough about the people's hardship without experience.
		7. Although King Edward studied every day, he could be good because he knew about suffering and oppression.
		8. Advisors can help a ruler to make good decisions when the education is not enough.

GOVERNMENT

Good rulers have to experience ordinary people's hardship because _____.
(Assertion)   (Reason)
For example, _____.
           (Evidence)

REASON	EVIDENCE

OPPOSITION

Good rulers do Not have to experience ordinary people's hardship because _____.
(Assertion)   (Reason)
For example, _____.
           (Evidence)

REASON	EVIDENCE

FORMAT TO DEBATE

Read and learn what points of information are.

Points of Information

In Parliamentary Debate formats, such as Asian Parliamentary Debate, debaters give points of information (POIs). A point of information is a question or statement presented by an opposing debater during a constructive speech. This is a good way for debaters to show how they disagree with the other team.

A debater can raise one hand and say, "Point of information." Then, the speaker can accept the point and answer the question.

However, speakers don't always have to accept a point of information from the other team. Sometimes, the speaker can reject the point. A POI should not be more than fifteen seconds in length and should be no more than two or three sentences.

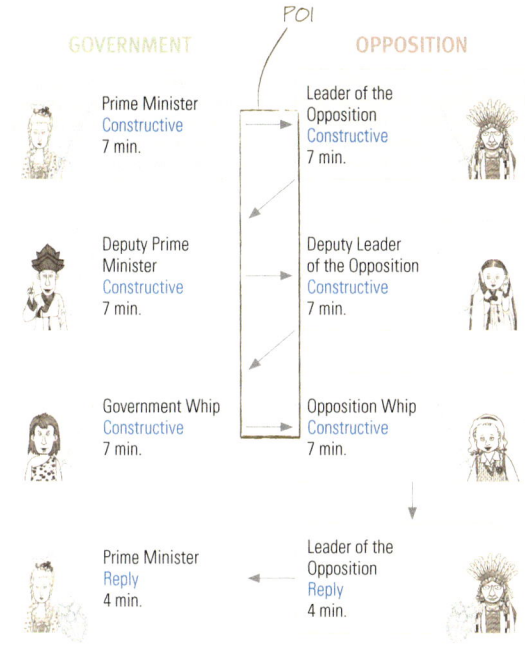

DEBATE KEYNOTES

Debaters never give points of information during a speech by a speaker on their own team.

APPLY TO DEBATE

Label the reason "R" and the evidence "E" for each side of the argument as well as the point of information "POI" by the other team. Then, with a partner, write an answer to the point of information.

Debate Topic: Rulers can only be good if they experience ordinary people's hardship.

GOVERNMENT	Answer to POI
1. Isn't education another way to learn how to make these solutions?	
2. Rulers learn how to make better political solutions by experiencing hardship.	
3. Edward created fair laws because he experienced the people's hardship.	

OPPOSITION	Answer to POI
1. Prince Edward had advisors to help him, and they continued to help him when he was king.	
2. Do you believe that all advisors can propose good solutions gained through experience?	
3. Rulers can also be good by relying on wise advisors.	

DEVELOP TO DEBATE

Insert the reasons and evidence from Argument to Debate into the chart in a logical order. Perform the debate in two groups.

Debate Topic: This house believes that **good rulers have to experience ordinary people's hardship.**

GOVERNMENT

Prime Minister's Constructive [First Affirmative Speech]

DEFINITION This debate argues that rulers should spend some time _____ before they are able to solve _____ *(actually live as an ordinary person, effectively)*

TEAM LINE Practical solutions to real problems only come through experience.

REASON _____ *(practical solutions)*

EVIDENCE _____

Deputy Prime Minister's Constructive [Second Affirmative Speech]

TEAM LINE _____

REBUTTAL What the other team said is not true. Education is simply not enough to learn about people's real problems.

REASON _____

EVIDENCE _____

Government Whip's Constructive [Third Affirmative Speech]

TEAM LINE _____

REBUTTAL What the other team said is not significant. Even advisors simply cannot provide enough information.

DETAIL King Henry VIII had _____ as Edward VI did, but Henry VIII _____ *(the same education, advisors, tyrant)*

Prime Minister's Reply [Affirmative Reply Speech]

TEAM LINE _____

REBUTTAL What the other team said is not significant. There may be many ways to learn lessons, but they are learned most effectively through experience.

THE BIG PICTURE We believe that _____ because rulers _____ *(most important skills, through experience)*

Debate Format

Asian Parliamentary Debate

OPPOSITION

Leader of the Opposition's Constructive [First Negative Speech]
TEAM LINE Experience is only one of many ways to learn valuable lessons.

REBUTTAL What the other team said is not significant. There are other ways to learn the same thing and get necessary knowledge.

REASON _____ (good education)

EVIDENCE

Deputy Leader of the Opposition's Constructive [Second Negative Speech]
TEAM LINE

REBUTTAL What the other team said is not always true. There are more ways to gain information, and some people have a significant knowledge beyond experience.

REASON

EVIDENCE

Opposition Whip's Constructive [Third Negative Speech]
TEAM LINE

REBUTTAL What the other team said is not always true. Even if experience is valuable, rulers can't experience every hardship people face.

DETAIL Edward only experienced _____

so _____ (for a short time, most of one's wisdom, education)

Leader of the Opposition's Reply [Negative Reply Speech]
TEAM LINE

REBUTTAL What the other team said is not true. Lessons learned from a variety of sources are even more effective.

THE BIG PICTURE We do not believe that _____

because _____

(education and advisors, learn the same lessons)

DEBATE CHAMPION TIP
Create Clash
To make your team's ideas stronger, try to show how your ideas are the opposite of the other team's ideas. It is easier for judges to see why you should win if your ideas are clearly opposite.

LESSON 6 DEBATE CURRENT ISSUES
6A SCHEMA CHAMPION

CRITIQUE TO DEBATE
• Free MP3 File Downloadable @www.LARRABEE.co.kr

Read the story carefully, paying special attention to the motives and behaviors of the people involved in the issue.

Beyond Native Teachers

Millions of people worldwide take classes to learn to speak English. They spend thousands of hours reading books, studying grammar, writing essays and practicing conversations to improve. Most of them think it is better to take English classes from a native English-speaking teacher who grew up speaking English. They think they can't learn English as well from a teacher who learned English as a teenager or adult.

However, many people are now **challenging** this idea. They say that students can learn at least as well from a teacher who had to study English just like the students. Some people even say that these teachers teach better than native speakers.

One reason is that non-native teachers understand the challenges students face better than native speakers do. These teachers had to invest a great deal of time and effort to learn English. They understand the students' language and culture better. They also understand the challenges and difficulties that students face when they try to understand a new language and culture better than native speakers do. This is important to students, as seventy percent of students prefer a teacher who understands their culture to a teacher who is a native English speaker.

Non-native teachers have experienced these challenges themselves, and they know how to solve them. They can teach effective ways to learn vocabulary, grammar and other language skills through practical **learning strategies**. These teachers can serve as a model for students to **motivate** them to succeed.

Also, non-native teachers know the rules of English in a clear and obvious way. Native speakers may know these same rules, but they may have trouble explaining them clearly. Native speakers often don't know which rules students find difficult and why. They may not be able to give the information students need. Because non-native speakers have had to learn everything **consciously**, they know which rules are difficult and appropriate for each level. They can help students find their proficiency* level and can easily explain their strengths and weaknesses as

*proficiency: how well someone does something

well as the typical patterns of errors these students make in the language learning process.

Of course, there are many ways for native speakers to gain a good knowledge of these. Classes for teaching English can explain rules so that native speakers understand them more consciously. Also, English speakers can study other foreign languages to make them more **aware of** the process of learning a second or foreign language. These steps can help native speakers to understand their students' challenges.

Another possibility for native English-speaking teachers is that non-native teachers, advisors or program directors can help them understand the rules and students' learning traits and feelings. Then, students can enjoy the advantages of learning from native speakers and also learn the information that non-native teachers could give.

Many programs also encourage native and non-native teachers to work together to plan lessons and teach students. Non-native teachers can explain everything to the students clearly. The native speakers can teach the students, giving them the advantage of an **authentic** model of **fluency** and pronunciation.

However, native English-speaking teachers cannot learn exactly how students feel in a class unless they go through the same challenges. They **are unlikely to** learn and remember all the rules that students need to know. Even studying another language does little to make native

speakers more aware of rules in their own native language.

Native speakers would need to spend a lot of time with non-native teachers to understand what students need to know. Additionally, unless these native speakers have studied another foreign language, they may never be able to understand the students' **anxiety** about the process of learning a foreign language.

Some students prefer to study English with a native English-speaking teacher, especially at higher levels. However, there can be many benefits from studying with non-native teachers. These teachers can identify with students more easily and clearly explain the information that is most challenging to students. Instead of favoring one group of teachers, students should learn to value all English teachers no matter what their native languages might be.

CUE TO DEBATE

Discuss the questions. Your answers will be a cue for your debate speech.

Do you think non-native teachers who had to study English as a second or foreign language teach the language more efficiently? Why or why not?

Why do you think some advanced students prefer to study English with a native English-speaking teacher?

BUILD TO DEBATE

Study the essential vocabulary for this lesson to build knowledge for debate.

1 LANGUAGE TO COMPREHEND
Choose the correct synonym for each word or phrase.

1. **challenging**   a. questioning   b. agreeing with   c. thinking about
2. **motivate**   a. inspire   b. force   c. discourage
3. **aware of**   a. ignorant of   b. comfortable with   c. knowing about
4. **authentic**   a. expensive   b. educated   c. real
5. **fluency**   a. speaking carefully b. speaking smoothly   c. listening quickly
6. **are unlikely to**   a. are capable of   b. probably won't   c. don't want to

2 LANGUAGE TO DEBATE
Choose the correct definition of each word or phrase.

1. Non-native speakers used many **learning strategies** to help them learn a foreign language.
   a. plans to learn   b. activities to study

2. Native speakers usually don't know the grammar rules of their language **consciously**.
   a. correctly   b. with awareness

3. Students are likely to experience **anxiety** in the process of language learning.
   a. anger   b. nervousness

THINK TO DEBATE

Think and share ideas to explore the debatable issues in the story. You may use the cues. You may need to change the form.

1 Why are non-native teachers better at explaining English easily?

• study • the same way students do

2 Why is it hard for native speakers to explain English clearly even if they take classes?

• rules • conciously

3 How can classes for teaching English help native speakers?

• understand • language learning process

4 How can non-native teachers help native speakers become better English teachers?

• explain • information

5 How can non-native teachers and native English-speaking teachers work together to teach students better?

• explanation • authentic • fluency

6 How does studying a foreign language help native English speakers become better teachers?

• aware of • process of learning

7 Why do you think many students prefer to have a teacher who understands their own culture?

• experiences • not be confused

8 Do you prefer to study English with a non-native English-speaking teacher or with a native English-speaking teacher? Why?

• understand • authentic

LESSON 6
DEBATE CURRENT ISSUES

6B DEBATE CHAMPION

ARGUMENT TO DEBATE

Label each part of the arguments. Use "R" for reasons, "E" for evidence, "P" for pro arguments and "C" for con arguments. Then, place the reasons and evidence on the correct side of the debate.

Resolution: Good teachers have to experience students' challenges.

PRO OR CON	REASON OR EVIDENCE	ARGUMENT CHAMPION
		1. Native speakers can take classes about teaching English to learn what learning strategies students need to use to learn English better.
		2. By experiencing challenges, teachers gain the ability to give practical solutions.
		3. Teachers cannot study and learn enough about the students' challenges without experience.
		4. Native speakers can ask for help from non-native teachers to learn how to help students solve their problems.
		5. With a good education, a teacher has all the information necessary to be a good teacher.
		6. Non-native teachers can explain ways to learn English more easily because they consciously had to learn everything the students learn.
		7. Even after taking classes, native speakers cannot understand students' anxiety in the language learning process.
		8. Advisors or program directors can help a teacher to make good decisions when the education is not enough.

TEAM A *PRO*

Good teachers have to experience students' challenges because _____. For example, _____.
(**A**ssertion) (**R**eason) (**E**vidence)

REASON	EVIDENCE

TEAM B *CON*

Good teachers do Not have to experience students' challenges because _____. For example, _____.
(**A**ssertion) (**R**eason) (**E**vidence)

REASON	EVIDENCE

RESEARCH TO DEBATE

Research the following questions to make your argument strong. You may use the cues.

1. What percentage of English teachers worldwide are non-native speakers? (Non-native English-speaking Teachers (NNESTs) percentage of teachers)
2. Why do many students prefer to study with non-native speakers? (benefits of non-native speaker teachers)
3. Why do some students prefer to study with native speakers? (benefits of native speaker teachers)

FORMAT TO DEBATE
Read and learn what crossfire is.

Crossfire

Crossfire is such an important part of Public Forum Debate that the format is sometimes known as Crossfire Debate. In every Public Forum Debate, there are three crossfire sessions. The first two are between the two speakers who just finished speaking, and all four speakers speak in the last crossfire, which is called the grand crossfire. The speaker who just finished speaking should always answer the first question in the crossfire.

Crossfire provides an opportunity for debaters to ask and answer questions. In this way, teams can try to challenge the arguments of the other side. It can also make it easier for the judges and the audience to see how the pro and con sides are different.

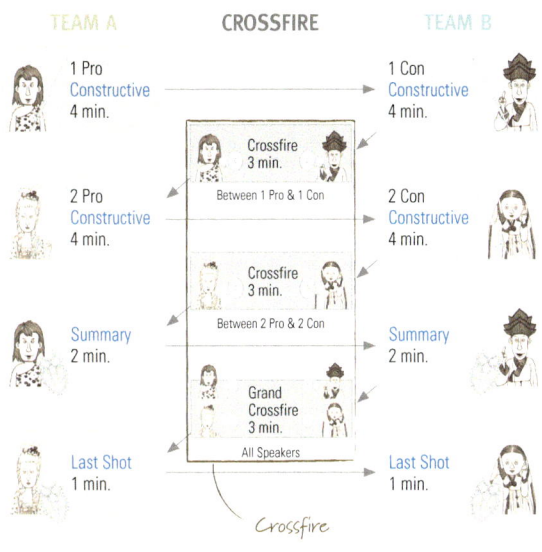

DEBATE KEYNOTES
Crossfire shows the judges and the audience exactly where the differences in each side's opinion are.

APPLY TO DEBATE
Read the reasons. Then choose the correct crossfire question and answer.

> Resolution: **Good teachers have to get a good education.**

PRO

REASON	With a good education, a teacher has all the information necessary to be a good teacher.
CROSSFIRE QUESTION	Q1. Why does a teacher need to have a good education?
	Q2. How can teachers teach effective ways to learn without the same experience as students?
CROSSFIRE ANSWER	A1. Books and classes on teaching strategies can give them vast information beyond their experience.
	A2. The teacher needs to get as much information as possible to help students solve their problems.

CON

REASON	By experiencing challenges, teachers gain the ability to give practical solutions.
CROSSFIRE QUESTION	Q1. Why are solutions from experience more practical than those from education?
	Q2. Why is it important for teachers to give practical solutions?
CROSSFIRE ANSWER	A1. Teachers can give practical solutions to all students if they experienced the students' challenges.
	A2. Solutions from experience are more practical because they solve both the feelings and the academic problems.

DEVELOP TO DEBATE

Insert the reasons and evidence from Argument to Debate into the chart in a logical order. Perform the debate in two groups. Instead of a coin toss, Pro team will begin.

Resolution:
Good teachers have to experience students' challenges.

TEAM A *PRO* CROSSFIRE

First Pro Constructive Speech

DEFINITION This debate says that teachers must learn _____ before they are able to _____ (as a student, effectively)

TEAM LINE Students' challenges can only be understood through experience.

REASON _____ (practical)

EVIDENCE _____

First Crossfire

Second Pro Constructive Speech

TEAM LINE _____

REBUTTAL What the other team said is not true. Education simply cannot provide enough information.

REASON _____

EVIDENCE _____

Second Crossfire

Summary Speech

TEAM LINE _____

REBUTTAL What the other team said is not significant. Native teachers cannot give enough information without the same experience as students.

DETAIL Many students prefer non-native teachers since they _____ (understand, explain clearly)

Grand Crossfire

The Last Shot

TEAM LINE _____

THE BIG PICTURE We agree that _____

because teachers _____ (not gain, from education OR practical solutions, experience)

DEBATE CHAMPION TIP

Speech Times and Preparation
In Public Forum Debate, the constructive speeches can take one minute. Each crossfire session can take about fifty seconds, and the summary speeches and last shots should take about thirty seconds. Each team has the opportunity to take up two minutes of preparation time during the debate.

Debate Format

Public Forum Debate

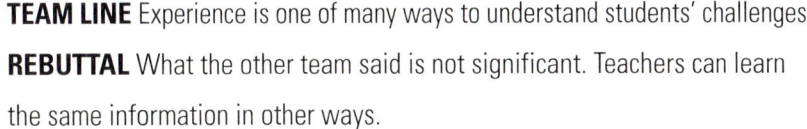

First Con Constructive Speech
TEAM LINE Experience is one of many ways to understand students' challenges.
REBUTTAL What the other team said is not significant. Teachers can learn the same information in other ways.
REASON ....
EVIDENCE ....

Second Con Constructive Speech
TEAM LINE ....
REBUTTAL What the other team said is not always true. Teachers can gain enough knowledge from a variety of sources, not only experience.
REASON ....
EVIDENCE .... (program directors)

Summary Speech
TEAM LINE ....
REBUTTAL What the other team said is not significant. Understanding students' challenges is not the most important quality teachers should have.
DETAIL There are some students who prefer native English-speaking teachers because ....
.... in the process of learning English. (fluency, pronunciation, important)

The Last Shot
TEAM LINE ....
THE BIG PICTURE We do not agree that ....

because ....
.... (education, the same knowledge OR advisors, the same knowledge)

CROSSFIRE TO DEBATE

Write the number of each question by the right speaker. You can also use your own ideas during the crossfire. Take turns to ask and answer completely and politely.

CROSSFIRE CHAMPION

① Is it possible for teachers to learn what an experience feels like through education?

② Why are solutions learned through experience more practical than those learned through education?

③ Is it always necessary to understand students' anxiety to help them learn a language?

④ How can advice from program directors or advisors substitute for experience to help teachers understand students' challenges?

LINK TO DEBATE
Read the situation below. Then, use strong arguments to become a debate champion.

SARAH'S DILEMMA

Sarah is planning to sign up for another English class because she really loves studying English. She wants to take a class about reading and discussing English literature. There are two different sections of the class, and they are taught by different teachers. One of the sections is taught by a native English speaker, Ralph. He doesn't have experience studying a foreign or a second language, but he has taught English for many years. The other section is taught by a non-native teacher, Amy. She is from Sarah's hometown. She has studied English for many years and lived abroad for several years. Everyone says her English is very good. Sarah isn't sure which section she should sign up for.

MY VOICE

Sarah has a significant choice to make. If she signs up for the class with the native speaker, the teacher may help her to speak English _____

(authentic way, pronunciation)

but he may not be able to _____

(understand, explain clearly)

In my opinion, good teachers [have to / do not have to] experience students' challenges because _____

For example, _____

Another reason is _____

For example, _____

I would urge her to consider these ideas.

68 UNIT 3 Debate Link

UNIT 4
Having More Knowledge Helps Us See the World More Clearly

Gulliver's Travels by Jonathan Swift
LITERATURE TO DEBATE

LISTEN TO DEBATE Track 7

Listen and number each box. Take notes while you listen and tell the story using the cues. You may need to change the form.

• pirates	• humans and horses	• be wrecked	• large people
• floating island	• in control	• powerful	• cute
• interesting ideas	• respect	• defeat	• keep ~ like a pet
• get away	• make ~ leave	• escape	• eagle

| LESSON 7 | Debate Literature | Gulliver's Travels | Asian Parliamentary Debate |
| LESSON 8 | Debate Current Issues | A Web of Information | Public Forum Debate |

LESSON 7

DEBATE LITERATURE

7A SCHEMA CHAMPION

READ TO DEBATE Track 8

Read the story carefully, paying special attention to the thoughts and behaviors of the main characters.

FACT FILE		
	Context	Based in England in the early 1700s, the main character visits the imaginary lands of Lilliput, Brobdingnag, Laputa and the land of the Houyhnhnms.
	Publication Date	The book was written between 1712 and 1726 in London and Dublin. It was published in London in 1726.
	Author	Jonathan Swift was an Irish writer and pastor. He lived from 1667 to 1745.
	Genre	Satire; Fantasy

Gulliver's Travels, by Jonathan Swift

Lemuel Gulliver* studied at Cambridge. After three years, he worked with a surgeon in London and learned his trade. After spending two and a half more years learning
5 about various kinds of medicine, Gulliver got a job working as a surgeon on a ship. For three and a half years he traveled in the Mediterranean. He spent six more years traveling around the world.

On one of these voyages*, Gulliver's ship
10 was wrecked on an island, and he was the only man to arrive on shore. After swimming through the stormy sea, Gulliver was so tired that he immediately fell asleep in the grass.

When Gulliver woke up, he found that he
15 was tied to the ground by many tiny threads, and he could not move. He felt a small creature walking on him, and as he looked down, he saw a very tiny human. The creature was less than six inches (15.24 cm) tall, and when Gulliver cried out, the human ran away as fast as he could. 20

Other such creatures also came. To protect themselves, they shot him with hundreds of arrows when he tried to pick one of them up, but the arrows were so small that they could hardly hurt him. Eventually, Gulliver made them realize 25 that he didn't want to hurt them.

He stuck his finger in his mouth to show that he wanted food. Then, many tiny ladders were placed against Gulliver's side, and the little men climbed up to his mouth with trays filled 30 with tiny pieces of meat and glasses of wine.

After feeding him and letting him rest, the tiny people built a large machine to carry Gulliver into the city. There, they introduced him

*In the original text, the main character, Lemuel Gulliver, tells the story from the first-person point of view looking back at his adventures.
*voyages: trips; experiences traveling

CHARACTER WEB

Lilliputians [lɪlpjuəʃəns]
a race of small people living in Lilliput

Blefuscudians [blefə́scudiəns]
a race of small people living in Blefuscu

The Emperor
the ruler of the Lilliputians

Brobdingnagians [brabdɪŋnǽgiəns]
a race of enormous people living in Brobdingnag

The Farmer
the giant who finds Gulliver

Glumdalclitch [glʌmdə́lglitʃ]
the farmer's daughter who takes care of Gulliver

The Queen
the wife of the king of Brobdingnag who buys Gulliver

Lemuel Gulliver protagonist

Laputans [ləpjutəns]
a race of scientific and mathematical scholars on the island of Laputa, Balnibarbi

Luggnaggians [lʌgnǽgiəns]
a race of people in the city of Luggnagg; some of whom are born to be immortal

Yahoos
a race of humans who serve the Houyhnhnms

Houyhnhnms [hǔinəms]
a race of horses who rule their land

---

to their emperor. At first, Gulliver was kept chained to a large building. Afterwards, he proved himself careful and trustworthy and was allowed to move about the city freely. However, he was carefully instructed never to hurt any of the people of that country on his journeys.

Now, the people of Lilliput, where Gulliver was living, were at war with the people of Blefuscu over the issue of whether eggs should be broken at the bigger end or the smaller end. When Blefuscu's naval **fleet** attacked Lilliput, Gulliver went to the sea to defend Lilliput and tied all the Blefuscan boats together with rope. Then, he stole the boats. However, Gulliver refused to take the Blefuscudians and make them into slaves, so it was the emperor's pleasure to put Gulliver's eyes out in punishment. Gulliver escaped from the emperor of Lilliput and fixed a boat to take him back to England.

Two months later, Gulliver left England again, but his ship ran out of fresh water. He and some other men were forced to go onto land in search of water. Not finding any, Gulliver turned to go back to the ship. At the shore, he saw that the other men were **fleeing from** a large animal and had already left in their boat.

Soon, Gulliver was found by a giant farmer who was 72 feet (21.9456 m) tall. He was one of a race of people called the Brobdingnagians. The farmer picked Gulliver up and then set him down on all fours*. Gulliver stood up and walked back and forth slowly to show the farmer that he would not run away. The farmer showed Gulliver to his family, and the family was very **amused** by him. They picked him up and looked at him and passed him around. Eventually, the farmer let his daughter, Glumdalclitch, take care of Gulliver, and she took care of him very well.

*all fours: arms and legs

The farmer decided to show Gulliver off to anyone who would pay to see him. Many people came, and Gulliver became very tired. He soon began to grow sick, and the farmer was afraid that Gulliver would soon die. When the queen saw Gulliver, she was amazed and happily bought Gulliver from the farmer. Gulliver was pleased to go with the queen. His only request was that Glumdalclitch might be allowed to go with him to the palace to take care of him.

Gulliver had an easy life at the palace, but he found it rather boring. He didn't like being around such enormous people, and he didn't even think the king was smart. The king didn't know anything at all about **politics**, and he couldn't begin to understand the uses of the cannon*.

Sometimes Gulliver had to escape from giant animals. He was chased by a giant wasp* one day, and on another occasion a giant monkey carried him up to the roof of the palace. All of this made Gulliver want to leave Brobdingnag, but he couldn't think of a good way to do it.

Then, one day, the royal family went on a trip, and Gulliver was taken in his carrying box, which was really a fine house full of furniture that seemed tiny to the Brobdingnagians but which was normal to Gulliver. Gulliver begged to be taken to the seashore and allowed to rest. The boy who took care of him set him down and apparently walked off because Gulliver then realized that he was flying through the air. An eagle had picked up his box and carried it for a while before dropping it into the sea.

Gulliver was at once picked up by sailors and taken back to England. He did not stay there long, though, before he decided to set sail again. After his ship was attacked by pirates, he was left on a lonely island near India. He had just decided that he was going to die on that lonely island when he saw an island floating through the sky.

Gulliver was rescued by the people of the floating island and was told that the island was called Laputa. Laputa was the capital city of a land called Balnibarbi. It floated over all the land and prevented any city from getting sunlight or rain unless it was obedient to the king of Laputa. If the land below was particularly **rebellious**, the Laputans threw rocks down onto the rebel city.

Gulliver found that the Laputans started thinking about other things so easily that they had to hire people to hit them while they were talking. It was the only way they could keep their minds on the conversation.

In the land of Balnibarbi, Gulliver saw that the Laputans were interested in studying math and science. They enjoyed doing almost any type of **experiments** so long as it was wholly useless. They worked hard to find out the best method for extracting light from cucumbers. They tried to turn ice into gunpowder. They even tried to learn the secret of building houses from the roof down instead of from the floor up.

Gulliver was quickly tired of these people, but, unable to leave the land as quickly as he wanted, he went to the city of Luggnagg to meet the Luggnaggians. There he found that there

---

*cannon: a type of very large gun on wheels
*wasp: an insect similar to a bee

were people who were born to be **immortal**, but they were not at all happy. These poor souls became depressed when they were thirty, and by the time they were eighty they were bitter and angry. There was no greater **curse** than to be born to be immortal.

Finally, Gulliver met a ship setting sail for Japan. He traveled from Japan to England. There he rested with his family for a time, but he left them again before much time had passed and headed out in his own ship. Unfortunately, Gulliver lost many men on his ship, and he was required to hire more men during the journey. These men led the crew to mutiny*, and Gulliver was abandoned in another unknown land.

Arriving in this land, Gulliver saw some creatures that looked almost human, but they had long hair and beards and long claws that they used to climb trees. Gulliver tried to find people there, but one of the creatures approached him instead. He hit the creature, and then a whole group of them attacked him. Gulliver hid away from the creatures.

After a while, Gulliver noticed a couple of horses nearby talking about him. They kept looking at him and saying "Yahoo." Then, they took him to a house. At the house, he saw many horses doing different activities. They continued to look at him and talk about him. Finally, they took him outside and stood him next to one of the creatures. Gulliver realized that the creature did seem very much like a human.

Slowly, Gulliver learned the ways of his new hosts. He realized that the horses were called Houyhnhnms, and they completely controlled the human-like Yahoos. The Yahoos were not good or kind creatures in any way, but the Houyhnhnms were **rational** and noble. Gulliver learned the Houyhnhnm language and spent many hours talking to the horses every day.

After some time, however, some of the Houyhnhnms decided that Gulliver was a lot like a Yahoo after all, and he was required to leave their land. Gulliver was upset, but he had no choice. A Portuguese ship came and picked him up in their boat. The captain was very kind to Gulliver and treated him well, but when Gulliver looked at him, he only saw an evil Yahoo.

Even after returning to his own country, Gulliver found that he thought of people as Yahoos. He even rejected his own family in favor of his horses and barely talked to his family for a year. Instead, he spent hours of every day in the barn talking to his horses.

*mutiny: revolt against the leader of a ship

CUE TO DEBATE

Discuss the questions. Your answers will be a cue for your debate speech.

Do you think the Laputans, who had the most knowledge, saw the world most clearly?

Do you think Gulliver was able to see the world more clearly than the groups of people he met on his journey?

BUILD TO DEBATE

Study the essential vocabulary for this lesson to build knowledge for debate.

1 LANGUAGE TO COMPREHEND
Choose the correct synonym for each word or phrase.

1. **fleet** — a. quick army   b. group of ships   c. strong weapon
2. **amused** — a. entertained   b. bored   c. annoyed
3. **politics** — a. science of government   b. science of weapons   c. science of business
4. **rebellious** — a. not resistant   b. not pleasant   c. not obedient
5. **immortal** — a. wicked   b. wealthy   c. eternal
6. **curse** — a. pleasant event   b. terrible thing   c. curious thing

2 LANGUAGE TO DEBATE
Choose the correct definition of each word or phrase.

1. In Lilliput, Gulliver met some very small **creature**.
   a. person or animal
   b. thing made by humans

2. Because Gulliver's shipmates were **fleeing from** an animal, they forgot about Gulliver.
   a. running away from
   b. moving from in a ship

3. The Laputans tried different types of **experiments**, but they all led to useless results.
   a. academic knowledge
   b. scientific tests

4. Gulliver liked the Houyhnhnms because they were **rational**.
   a. logical
   b. careful

74 UNIT 4 LESSON 7 Debate Literature

THINK TO DEBATE

Think and share ideas to explore the debatable issues in the story. You may use the cues. You may need to change the form.

1 How did the Lilliputians react when they first saw Gulliver?

• afraid • tie ~ down

2 Why did the Lilliputians decide to let Gulliver move about the city freely?

• not hurt • careful

3 Why did the Lilliputians fight with the Blefuscudians? Was it an important argument?

• break eggs • bigger or smaller

4 What knowledge did the Brobdingnagians have? Did this help them see the world clearly?

• not much information

5 Why did the Laputans waste their time on useless experiments?

• knowledge • practical

6 Why didn't the Laputans recognize that their experiments were useless?

• not know • any other experiments

7 Were the Laputans good at holding a conversation? Why or why not?

• thoughtful • not keep one's mind

8 Why did Gulliver spend so much time in the barn after he came back to England the last time?

• respect • hate

Gulliver's Travels, by Jonathan Swift 7A 75

LESSON 7
DEBATE LITERATURE

7B DEBATE CHAMPION

ARGUMENT TO DEBATE
Label each part of the arguments. Use "R" for reasons, "E" for evidence, "G" for government arguments and "O" for opposition arguments. Then, place the reasons and evidence on the correct side of the debate.

Debate Topic: Having more knowledge helps us see the world more clearly.

GOVERNMENT OR OPPOSITION	REASON OR EVIDENCE	ARGUMENT CHAMPION
		1. Sometimes with more information we still seek useless ends.
		2. Having more knowledge can also mislead us so that we evaluate the world incorrectly.
		3. The Laputans had more information, but their information and experiments were useless.
		4. Through more knowledge, we can recognize what is not necessary.
		5. Gulliver had enough knowledge to recognize that the Laputans had useless experiments.
		6. Although Gulliver had a lot of knowledge about horses and people, his knowledge of the Yahoos and Houyhnhnms made him think that horses were better and more rational than people.
		7. At first the Lilliputians were afraid of Gulliver because they didn't know what kind of creature he was, but after they gained knowledge, they realized that he was careful and wouldn't flee from them.
		8. Gaining knowledge allows us to reevaluate previous ideas.

GOVERNMENT

Having more knowledge helps us see the world more clearly because _____.
(Assertion)   (Reason)
For example, _____.
(Evidence)

REASON	EVIDENCE

OPPOSITION

Having more knowledge does NOT help us see the world more clearly because _____.
(Assertion)   (Reason)
For example, _____.
(Evidence)

REASON	EVIDENCE

FORMAT TO DEBATE
Read and learn how to create an argument.

Assertion, Reason, Evidence

The basic element of any debate is the arguments, and arguments are made of assertions, reasons and evidence. An assertion is a clear statement of the main idea of one side of the debate. It is what you want to prove. Reasons explain why your side of the debate is right. Evidence shows that it is true. Good reasons make it possible for the audience and judges to believe your assertion, and evidence makes your reasons strong and more convincing.

There are many types of evidence that can be used in debate. We can use evidence from what we read or from our personal experience. We can also use evidence that everyone acknowledges as true. Often, it is valuable to state reasons more than once in slightly different ways. It is beneficial to provide many diverse types of evidence for each reason. If the evidence is good, it will make your whole argument strong and believable.

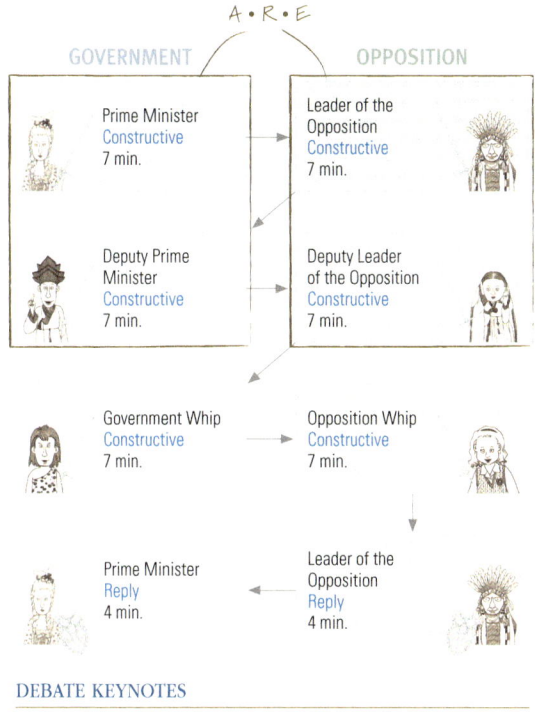

DEBATE KEYNOTES
Evidence can also be called supports and proof.

APPLY TO DEBATE
Read the debate topic and create an argument. Write an assertion, reason and evidence. Use your personal experience or reading to create your new evidence. Compare your work with a partner. Whose argument is stronger? Explain why.

Debate Topic: Having more knowledge helps us see the world more clearly.

ARGUMENT

ASSERTION

REASON

EVIDENCE

DEVELOP TO DEBATE

Insert the reasons and evidence from Argument to Debate into the chart in a logical order. Perform the debate in two groups.

Debate Topic: This house believes that **having more knowledge helps us see the world more clearly.**

GOVERNMENT

Prime Minister's Constructive [First Affirmative Speech]

DEFINITION This debate argues not only that knowledge is valuable for _____ but also that _____ (see and understand, the world, more knowledge)

TEAM LINE The more knowledge we have, the easier it is to understand the world.

REASON _____ (not necessary)

EVIDENCE _____

Deputy Prime Minister's Constructive [Second Affirmative Speech]

TEAM LINE _____

REBUTTAL What the other team said is not significant. It is possible to check to ensure that we are not turning to useless ends and that we evaluate ideas correctly.

REASON _____

EVIDENCE _____

Government Whip's Constructive [Third Affirmative Speech]

TEAM LINE _____

REBUTTAL What the other team said is not relevant. Although knowledge may mislead us, the only way to fight misleading knowledge is with accurate knowledge.

DETAIL Because of Gulliver's knowledge, he knew that it was _____ (not necessary, to fight over, break eggs)

Prime Minister's Reply [Affirmative Reply Speech]

TEAM LINE _____

REBUTTAL What the other team said is not relevant. More knowledge allows us to find our way out of any confusion.

THE BIG PICTURE We believe that _____ because we can better _____ (unnecessary, reevaluate)

78 UNIT 4 LESSON 7 Debate Literature

Debate Format

Asian Parliamentary Debate

OPPOSITION

Leader of the Opposition's Constructive [First Negative Speech]

TEAM LINE More knowledge can lead to more confusion.

REBUTTAL What the other team said is not always true. More knowledge also makes it possible to misunderstand the world and seek useless ends.

REASON _____ (seek)

EVIDENCE _____

Deputy Leader of the Opposition's Constructive [Second Negative Speech]

TEAM LINE _____

REBUTTAL What the other team said is not always true. We can use knowledge to help us, but we are just as likely to use it incorrectly, misleading us.

REASON _____

EVIDENCE _____

Opposition Whip's Constructive [Third Negative Speech]

TEAM LINE _____

REBUTTAL What the other team said is not significant. Although accurate knowledge can be helpful, people don't often use it well.

DETAIL The Laputans had _____ but they were so busy _____ that they couldn't even _____ (information, other things, focus on)

Leader of the Opposition's Reply [Negative Reply Speech]

TEAM LINE _____

REBUTTAL What the other team said is not true. Past a certain amount of knowledge, more knowledge is simply not helpful and leads to useless ends.

THE BIG PICTURE We do not believe that _____ because we _____ and still _____ (be misled, useless ends)

DEBATE CHAMPION TIP

Time to Prepare

In Asian Parliamentary Debate, teams have a few minutes before the debate to prepare for the debate. Spend five minutes with your team before the debate to think of any other reasons, evidence and rebuttals that your team can use to make your team's arguments.

LESSON 8: DEBATE CURRENT ISSUES

8A SCHEMA CHAMPION

CRITIQUE TO DEBATE
• Free MP3 File Downloadable @www.LARRABEE.co.kr

Read the story carefully, paying special attention to the motives and behaviors of the people involved in the issue.

A Web of Information

The introduction of the Internet has been one of the most important changes worldwide in the past few decades. As the Internet gained popularity in the mid 1990s, people were excited about their increased **access to** all kinds of information. Over time, people began to become concerned that people might suffer from too much information. It seemed that too much knowledge might lead people to wrong ideas or impressions.

The effect of the Internet on the political process was of **particular** concern to many people. People began to wonder how the Internet might affect important elections. They wondered if the Internet would help people access more true and fair information, or if people would believe every untrue or extreme idea.

For many years, the Internet seemed to play a relatively small role in elections. People shared ideas with their friends or visited political websites, but these were infrequent activities. Only a few people found political ideas or news online every day.

With the 2008 U.S. presidential election, it was clear that this had changed. More than half of adult Americans were going online to get information about the election. People were getting more information online than ever before, and they were also getting more information than ever before. Some of that information came directly from **candidates** or online versions of traditional news sources. Much of the information came from online blogs, video sharing sites or **social networking sites**.

Before the election, there were many websites for and against both Barack Obama and John McCain. Barack Obama hoped to become president as a member of the Democratic party, and John McCain wanted to become president for the Republican party. It would seem that people could learn all of the true information about both candidates. Indeed, that was possible, but more often, people found more positive information about the candidate they liked. However, they mostly looked at **negative** information about the candidate they didn't like.

Much of this online information was not true. Several false rumors became very popular online. In fact, about ninety percent of online Americans heard the untrue rumor that Obama was a Muslim. Many other rumors were heard by at least half of Americans, and many Americans believed them.

However, along with untrue information, the Internet also spread the truth about the candidates. Many Americans did not simply believe the information they heard. They kept searching to find out the truth behind the information. When they saw these rumors online, they also found facts showing that the rumors were not true and realized that they were mistaken. Further, although people spread many false rumors, they did not spread all of them. They only spread the rumors that seemed believable to them.

In addition to factual information from blogs, news sources and social networking sites, people also spent a lot of time watching videos or looking at other entertaining materials about the candidates. One of the most popular online videos was by "Obama girl." Obama girl was a model who made a music video about how much she liked Barack Obama. The video was shown on national news and made Obama more popular with some people. The video did not give any true or untrue information but was just for fun. Of course, most people recognized that videos like this should not change their opinions. They tried to find other information to help them make a rational decision about whom to vote for.

In the future, the Internet is likely to be an even more critical part of the political process. In 2010, seventy-five percent of Americans found political information online, and the percentage is likely to be even larger in 2012. The Internet is here to stay, and for better or worse, it gives people much more information about political candidates more quickly than ever before.

CUE TO DEBATE

Discuss the questions. Your answers will be a cue for your debate speech.

Do you think the Internet gave Americans better information to make better decisions?

Do you think people who had more knowledge made smarter choices?

BUILD TO DEBATE

Study the essential vocabulary for this lesson to build knowledge for debate.

1 LANGUAGE TO COMPREHEND
Choose the correct synonym for each word or phrase.

1. **access to**	a. exit to	b. hope to hear	c. ability to get
2. **particular**	a. special	b. common	c. picky
3. **social networking sites**	a. places to go with friends	b. time to meet friends	c. websites to meet friends
4. **factual**	a. fact-based	b. relevant	c. invented
5. **sources**	a. important papers	b. authority	c. places with information
6. **vote for**	a. criticize	b. choose	c. admire

2 LANGUAGE TO DEBATE
Choose the correct definition of each word or phrase.

1. Some people spread many false rumors about the **candidates** they didn't like.
   a. people voting
   b. people who can be chosen

2. Most people search for **negative** information about people they don't like.
   a. optimistic
   b. unpleasant

3. People realized that they were **mistaken** after they found more information online.
   a. confused
   b. ignorant

THINK TO DEBATE

Think and share ideas to explore the debatable issues in the story. You may use the cues. You may need to change the form.

1. What were the first effects of the Internet on politics?

• share ideas • political websites

2. Why do you think most people looked at positive information about their favorite candidate and negative information about the candidate they didn't like?

• already • make sure

3. Why did people hear so many rumors in 2008?

• travel fast online • a lot of information

4. Do you think the rumors led many people to make bad decisions? Why or why not?

• not believe • true information

5. Why do you think people mostly only shared information that they thought was believable?

• good decisions • not want to confuse

6. If you saw a rumor online, would you try to find more information to see if it was true? Why or why not?

• good decisions • not change one's mind

7. What were some online sources of election information in 2008?

• candidates • blogs

8. Why do you think so many people watched the "Obama girl" video?

• entertaining • not change one's opinion

LESSON 8
DEBATE CURRENT ISSUES

8B DEBATE CHAMPION

ARGUMENT TO DEBATE
Label each part of the arguments. Use "R" for reasons, "E" for evidence, "P" for pro arguments and "C" for con arguments. Then, place the reasons and evidence on the correct side of the debate.

Resolution: Having more knowledge helps us make better decisions.

PRO OR CON	REASON OR EVIDENCE	ARGUMENT CHAMPION
		1. Because people had access to a lot of knowledge, they could recognize that the "Obama girl" video was useless for making decisions.
		2. Even with more information, we still only pay attention to the idea we like.
		3. Although Americans heard many false rumors, they found the truth behind the information and realized they were mistaken.
		4. Most people only looked at positive information about the candidate they liked and negative information about the candidate they didn't like.
		5. Through more knowledge, we can recognize what is useless.
		6. Because there was so much information, many Americans heard and believed false rumors about the candidates.
		7. Gaining knowledge allows us to find out the truth about the information.
		8. Having more knowledge can also lead us to evaluate the world incorrectly.

TEAM A PRO

Having more knowledge helps us make better decisions because _____.
(Assertion)   (Reason)
For example, _____.
(Evidence)

REASON	EVIDENCE

TEAM B CON

Having more knowledge does NOT help us make better decisions because _____.
(Assertion)   (Reason)
For example, _____.
(Evidence)

REASON	EVIDENCE

RESEARCH TO DEBATE
Research the following questions to make your argument strong. You may use the cues.

1. How has the Internet affected elections in other countries? (effect of Internet elections in the U.K. / France / Korea / India)
2. What was the effect of mass media on elections? (mass media's effect on elections)
3. How are social networking sites changing election campaigns? (social networking elections)

FORMAT TO DEBATE
Read and learn how to research for debate.

The 3Rs: Relevant, Reliable, Recent

Research is an important part of debate because it supplies reasons and evidence. When you start to research, make a list of questions about your topic. This will help you find the information that is relevant to your topic because only that information can be useful to you.

It is important to make sure that your research comes from reliable sources. Statistics and expert opinions make good evidence, and it is often fairly easy to find out if they are true. This kind of information can often be found in good newspapers, and many government organizations have information about current topics online. Libraries might have useful books by academic writers. Debaters should always check to ensure that this information is recent. Search engines can also be useful. Some search engines have a special section for students and scholars with academic research. By looking in these places, it is possible to find recent research from experts.

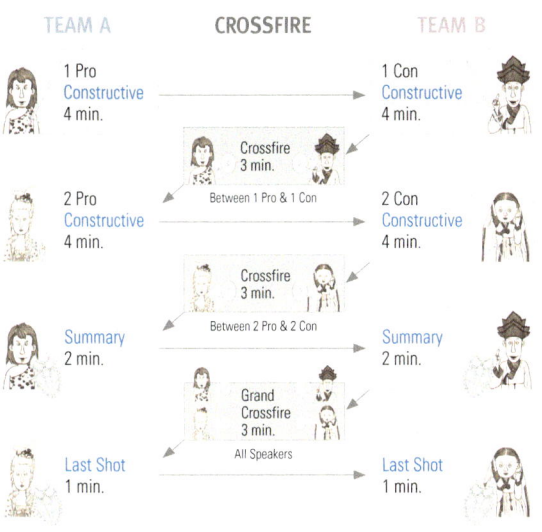

DEBATE KEYNOTES

The most recent information is always most believable in debates about current events.

APPLY TO DEBATE
Write two questions to research about the resolution below. Then, provide a good source for each answer and complete the research checklist.

Resolution: Having more knowledge helps us make smarter choices.

RESEARCH QUESTION	RESEARCH CHECKLIST
What percentage of people find election information online?	☑ Relevant
ANSWER BASED ON SOURCE	
Fourteen percent of Americans found election information online in 2000.	☑ Reliable
Title: *Internet Election News Audience Seeks Convenience, Familiar Names*	☐ Recent
Date: *Dec. 3, 2000* Author: *Andrew Kohut, Lee Rainie*	

RESEARCH QUESTION	RESEARCH CHECKLIST
	☐ Relevant
ANSWER BASED ON SOURCE	
	☐ Reliable
Title: Date: Author:	☐ Recent

A Web of Information 8B

DEVELOP TO DEBATE

Insert the reasons and evidence from Argument to Debate into the chart in a logical order. Perform the debate in two groups. Instead of a coin toss, Pro team will begin.

> **Resolution:**
> Having more knowledge helps us make better decisions.

TEAM A PRO — CROSSFIRE

First Pro Constructive Speech

DEFINITION This debate says not only that knowledge _____ but also that with more knowledge, _____
(helpful, decisions, smarter)

TEAM LINE Knowledge leads to better understanding and better decisions.

REASON _____ *(useless)*

EVIDENCE _____

First Crossfire

Second Pro Constructive Speech

TEAM LINE _____

REBUTTAL What the other team said is not always true. More information gives us the opportunity to find the truth about all types of information.

REASON _____

EVIDENCE _____

Second Crossfire

Summary Speech

TEAM LINE _____

REBUTTAL What the other team said is not relevant. If some knowledge misleads us, we should gather more information to make a wise decision.

DETAIL People who wanted to _____ were able to find it and use it to _____
(information, make an educated decision)

Grand Crossfire

The Last Shot

TEAM LINE _____

THE BIG PICTURE We agree that _____

because we _____
(identify, true information OR recognize, useful)

DEBATE CHAMPION TIP

The Split

In a debate competition, each debate contains many reasons, and they all have to be given in the two constructive speeches. The reasons have to be divided logically by topic or category, and both debaters should have an equal number of good reasons.

Debate Format

Public Forum Debate

TEAM B CON

First Con Constructive Speech

TEAM LINE The results of more knowledge are not at all consistent.

REBUTTAL What the other team said is not always true. We can't make a rational decision if the knowledge is biased.

REASON

EVIDENCE

Second Con Constructive Speech

TEAM LINE

REBUTTAL What the other team said is not always true. More knowledge does not always lead us to seek truth.

REASON

EVIDENCE

Summary Speech

TEAM LINE

REBUTTAL What the other team said is not significant. More knowledge can be useful, but many people choose not to use it wisely.

DETAIL Some people allowed _____ to influence _____ (useless, Obama girl, decisions)

The Last Shot

TEAM LINE

THE BIG PICTURE We do not agree that _____

because people _____ (only a part of OR incorrectly)

CROSSFIRE TO DEBATE

Write the number of each question by the right speaker. You can also use your own ideas during the crossfire. Take turns to ask and answer completely and politely.

CROSSFIRE CHAMPION

① What percent of people actually tried to find out the truth behind the information?

② Is it reasonable to say that people only saw positive information about the candidate they liked and never saw other information?

③ If people recognized that the "Obama girl" video was useless, why did it become more popular than useful information?

④ Do you think that these people would not have heard and believed false rumors if there had been less information?

A Web of Information 8B

LINK TO DEBATE
Read the situation below. Then, use strong arguments to become a debate champion.

DAVE'S DILEMMA

Dave wants to be the next student body president at his school. Some of the students already know a lot about him, but a lot of the students who will be voting in the election have never met Dave. Dave knows that he has to give them information about himself so that they can recognize that he will do the most for the school, but he isn't sure how much information to give. He might just tell people about his basic ideas, or he might make a website to explain all kinds of information about himself and his ideas for the school. Dave just wants to make sure that whatever he does will help students to choose him as the best student body president.

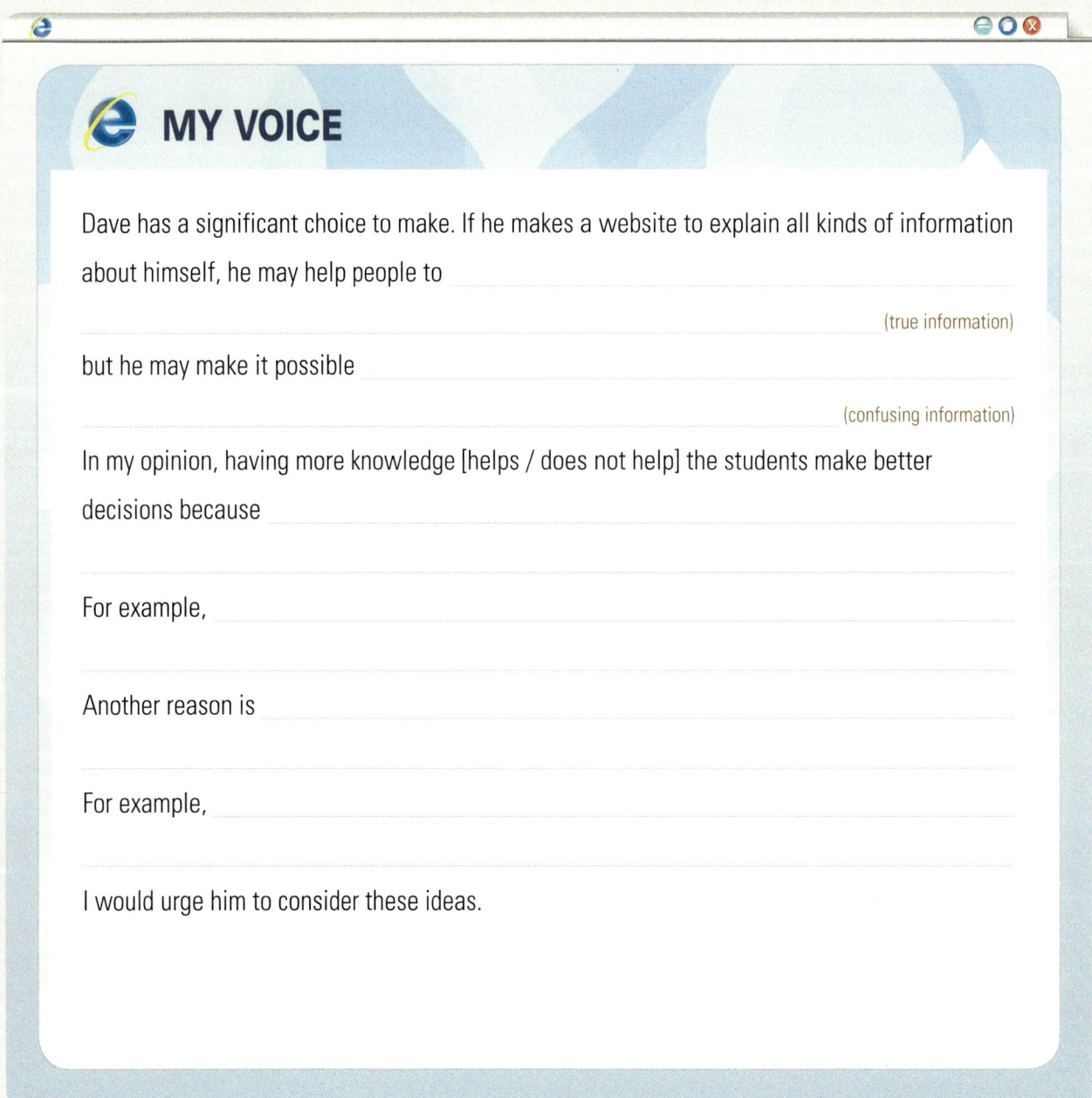

MY VOICE

Dave has a significant choice to make. If he makes a website to explain all kinds of information about himself, he may help people to _____

(true information)

but he may make it possible _____

(confusing information)

In my opinion, having more knowledge [helps / does not help] the students make better decisions because _____

For example, _____

Another reason is _____

For example, _____

I would urge him to consider these ideas.

UNIT 5: Scientists Should Always Be Responsible for the Consequences of Their Inventions

Frankenstein by Mary Shelley
LITERATURE TO DEBATE

LISTEN TO DEBATE — Track 9

Listen and number each box. Take notes while you listen and tell the story using the cues. You may need to change the form.

- creature
- give ~ life
- come to life
- too big and very ugly

- get married
- shoot
- chase
- ship

- partner
- worry about
- half-made
- kill

- little brother
- monster
- hate
- punish

| LESSON 9 | Debate Literature | Frankenstein | Asian Parliamentary Debate |
| LESSON 10 | Debate Current Issues | An Atomic Problem | Public Forum Debate |

LESSON 9

DEBATE LITERATURE

9A SCHEMA CHAMPION

READ TO DEBATE Track 10

Read the story carefully, paying special attention to the thoughts and behaviors of the main characters.

FACT FILE		
	Context	Most of the story takes place in Switzerland in the 1700s, although some segments occur in Britain and on the northern ice.
	Publication Date	The book was written between 1816 and 1817 in Switzerland and London. It was published in London in 1818.
	Author	Mary Shelley was an English writer. She was married to the English poet Percy Bysshe Shelley. Her parents were the philosopher William Godwin and the feminist Mary Wollstonecraft. She lived from 1797 to 1851.
	Genre	Gothic Horror; Science Fiction (one of the earliest examples of Science Fiction)

Frankenstein, by Mary Shelley

Victor Frankenstein was born in Geneva, and his family was wealthy and prosperous. He was the oldest of three sons. His parents were kind and generous, and when he was five years old, his mother brought home Elizabeth, a young orphan girl, to live with the family. No human being could have passed a happier childhood than Victor.

When Victor had finished his studies in Geneva, he decided to attend university at Ingolstadt. Not long before he left, Elizabeth **contracted** scarlet fever*, and Victor's mother also became ill from the same disease. Elizabeth fully recovered, but Victor's mother was not so fortunate. Victor had to delay his entrance to university to help the family adjust after his mother died.

At university, Victor was very interested in natural philosophy and chemistry, and he began at once to study with great eagerness. He was not afraid to study anything and to study it with his whole heart. He studied all the causes of the changes from life to death and death to life. Then, suddenly, he was able to put these ideas together in a completely new way. He knew what caused life, and, in fact, he became able to give life to something that was dead.

After discovering such an amazing secret, Victor worked hard to make a body. He took old body parts from different places and carefully stitched them together. He worked tirelessly night and day for two years. He didn't meet friends, visit family or even get enough sleep. He was in a state of **feverish** excitement waiting for

*scarlet fever: a disease that causes severe fever and red marks on the skin

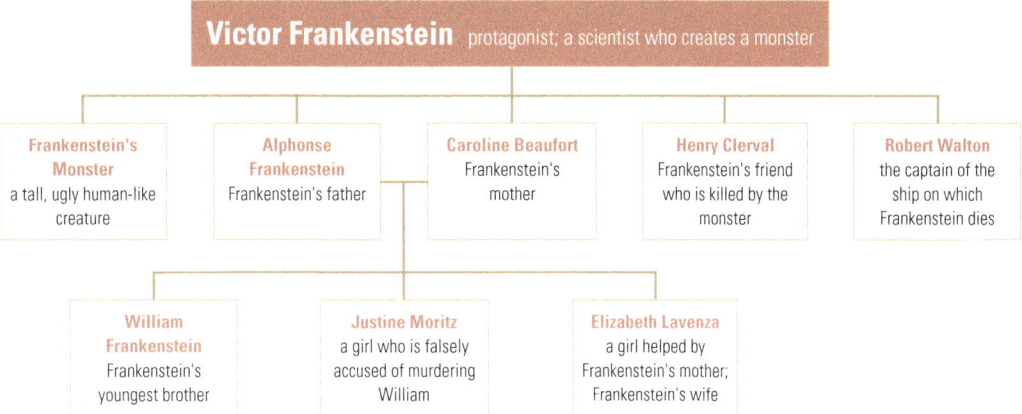

the day when he could see if he could create life. He predicted that giving life to the creature would be an amazing scientific development.

Late one November night, in an inner room of his apartment, he finally gave the creature life. He had chosen beautiful features for the creature. It had flowing black hair and pearly white teeth, but it also had thin yellow skin and watery eyes. When Victor saw the creature move, horror and disgust filled his heart.

Victor couldn't sleep well that night. The monster seemed to be looking at him, and Victor already regretted creating him. The next morning, Victor went out into the streets to look for his friend, and while he was gone, the creature also left the apartment. Soon, Victor became ill, and his friend took care of him in his apartment for several months until he was better.

When he recovered from his illness, Victor received a letter from his father. It said that Victor's youngest brother William had been murdered. Victor hurried back to Geneva to comfort his family. He arrived at Geneva just after dark, after the city gates had been closed.

He stayed in a village that night, and while he was taking a walk outside the village, a flash of lightning showed him a strange creature. The creature was uglier than any human, and Victor instantly knew that it was the monster to whom he had given life. He realized that this monster was also the murderer of his brother.

Victor finally arrived home, and his father told him that Justine, the kind girl who took care of Victor's brother, was accused of murdering the boy. A locket* that the boy had was found in Justine's pocket. She said that she didn't kill the boy. She said she had been sleeping, but no one believed her. Justine was

---

*locket: a piece of jewelry that you wear around your neck and in which you can put a picture, etc.

punished with death. This made Victor even more upset because his monster had killed two people who were like family to him.

Victor decided that he needed to take a break, and he went to the mountains to rest. One day, as he was walking over a mountain, he saw the figure of a man. It was moving towards him much faster than a man could walk. It leaped over large cracks in the ice and seemed taller than a man. When he saw it better, he knew it was the monster he had created. He shouted at the creature to go away, but the creature didn't go.

The monster said, "All men hate what is **miserable**, and I must be hated most because I'm the most miserable. You, my creator, hate me, your creature, even though our relationship is not so easily destroyed. If you create a woman for me to love, we will go to South America and live away from people. If you do not, I will kill all of your remaining friends."

Then, the monster told Victor about his life so far. He said that at first everyone had run away from him because he was ugly, and he had left Ingerstoldt. Then, he had lived near a family in the forest. He had learned that the man was blind, so he went to talk to him. The man could not see him and was not afraid of him. The old man enjoyed the monster's company, and at his house he learned how to read and how people behave. One day, the old man's family had returned to the house earlier than expected. Seeing the monster, they had become frightened and had driven him out of the house with stones.

Before the monster had left Victor's house, he had looked in the office and found some notes with Victor's name and hometown written on them. Feeling very lonely, the monster had gone towards Victor's hometown. While outside the town, he saw a small boy playing. He thought that the boy might be too young to hate the monster. The monster wanted the boy to be his friend and grabbed him to take him with him. However, the boy cried out and refused to go. He said that his name was Frankenstein. The monster, filled with anger at the sound of the name, caught the boy's throat and strangled* him until he was dead. Finding a locket on the boy, he took it off and put it in Justine's pocket so that people would think she killed him.

After hearing the whole story, Victor agreed to make a woman for the monster so that he would not kill all of his friends. Victor went to England and began again to create a body. When he was about half finished, he worried that the two monsters may not leave people alone. They may themselves have children, and their **descendants** could fill people with **terror** forever. He became afraid that people of the future might curse him for creating this woman.

Suddenly, he looked out the window and saw the monster there, watching him work. He decided that he could not create another monster, and he destroyed the half-made woman. The monster became incredibly angry and came into the room. He asked Victor why he had broken his promise and threatened him in every way

---

*strangled: killed someone by squeezing the neck

possible. Then, he said, "I will go as you said; but remember, I shall be with you on your wedding-night." That night, Victor went out onto a lake and dumped the second creature's body. However, he couldn't return to land that night and slept in the boat. In the morning, he went back to land and found the police waiting for him. They accused him of murdering his friend Henry whom he had traveled with and showed him the body. Victor saw the marks of the monster's fingers on his friend's neck. Again, the monster had killed someone Victor loved. Victor again became very ill.

When Victor was better, he went back to Geneva and married Elizabeth. The two went on their honeymoon. Victor thought the monster wanted to murder him on his wedding night, so he went out of their hotel room to search for the monster and attack the monster first. While he was out of the room, he heard a **shrill** and dreadful scream. He ran back to the room and saw his wife lying on the bed, completely lifeless. The monster had strangled her.

Victor looked up and saw the monster outside the window. He tried to shoot him, and a whole group of people ran after him. The monster ran away and jumped into a lake. They never did catch him.

The honeymoon was cut short, and Victor returned to his father's house. He told his father what happened, and the old man became very ill and soon died. Victor now felt free to chase the monster and get revenge. His life was now almost as miserable as the monster's life.

Victor followed the monster to the north. He got a dogsled and chased the monster further and further. He almost caught him, but then the ice broke. There was a huge crack in the ice between Victor and the monster. Then, Victor saw a ship trying to go to the North Pole. He was sick and hungry and agreed to travel on the ship.

Once on the ship, Victor seemed to get better, and he told the captain, Robert Walton*, the story of the terrible and ugly monster. Soon after Victor finished telling the story, his sickness finally killed him. A few days later, the captain heard a strange noise in the room where Victor was lying dead. He looked in and saw Frankenstein's monster crying out **in grief** and horror.

The monster told the captain that he would soon die, too. This creature did not wish to live longer than his creator. He would continue going north, and there he would die. The monster jumped out of the window of the room and landed on a large piece of floating ice beside the ship. He was carried away by the waves until the captain couldn't see him anymore.

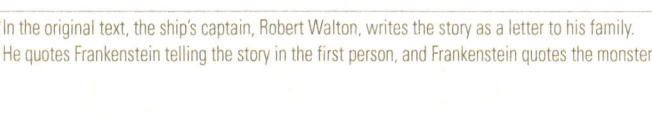

*In the original text, the ship's captain, Robert Walton, writes the story as a letter to his family. He quotes Frankenstein telling the story in the first person, and Frankenstein quotes the monster.

CUE TO DEBATE
Discuss the questions. Your answers will be a cue for your debate speech.

Do you think Frankenstein should have made a partner for the monster?

Do you think people should have punished Frankenstein for making the monster?

BUILD TO DEBATE
Study the essential vocabulary for this lesson to build knowledge for debate.

1 LANGUAGE TO COMPREHEND
Choose the correct synonym for each word or phrase.

1. **contracted** — a. kept in touch with   b. became ill with   c. treated

2. **feverish** — a. with little energy   b. long-lasting   c. with strong emotion

3. **was accused of** — a. was asked about   b. was seen   c. was blamed for

4. **descendants** — a. the people in earlier generations   b. the people in later generations   c. the people in the same generations

5. **shrill** — a. having a very high sound   b. having scary music   c. having a big laugh

6. **in grief** — a. sorrowfully   b. because of a wound   c. angrily

2 LANGUAGE TO DEBATE
Choose the correct definition of each word or phrase.

1. Frankenstein **predicted** that his invention would turn out well.
   a. doubted   b. expected

2. Frankenstein wanted to get revenge on his brother's **murderer**.
   a. person who dies   b. person who kills

3. Frankenstein's monster was **miserable** because he didn't have any friends.
   a. thrilled   b. unhappy

4. The monster filled everyone with **terror** because it was ugly.
   a. great fear   b. nightmare

94 UNIT 5 LESSON 9 Debate Literature

THINK TO DEBATE

Think and share ideas to explore the debatable issues in the story. You may use the cues. You may need to change the form.

1 What problems did Frankenstein's monster cause?

• kill • family

2 Why did Frankenstein start to create a partner for the monster?

• save • solve problems

3 How was the creature different from what Frankenstein expected it to be?

• beautiful features • turn to evil

4 Why did Frankenstein destroy the partner's half-made body?

• results • responsibility

5 Why did Frankenstein's monster turn to evil and become cruel?

• be mean to • feel rejected

6 Why did Frankenstein choose to make a creature?

• science • amazing invention

7 How did Frankenstein try to stop his monster?

• partner • shoot

8 Do you think Frankenstein could have done anything else to keep the monster from killing his family? Why or why not?

• befriend • stronger than

**LESSON 9
DEBATE LITERATURE**

9B DEBATE CHAMPION

ARGUMENT TO DEBATE

Label each part of the arguments. Use "R" for reasons, "E" for evidence, "G" for government arguments and "O" for opposition arguments. Then, place the reasons and evidence on the correct side of the debate.

Debate Topic: Scientists should always be responsible for the consequences of their inventions.

GOVERNMENT OR OPPOSITION	REASON OR EVIDENCE	ARGUMENT CHAMPION
		1. Inventions can cause serious harm if scientists make the wrong decision.
		2. Frankenstein believed that the creature would be beautiful, but later it turned out to be a monster and was miserable.
		3. Frankenstein made the wrong decision when he created a monster, and the monster became a murderer and killed many people.
		4. Scientists cannot predict how their inventions will turn out in the end.
		5. Scientists are the best ones to create a solution to problems they create.
		6. Frankenstein's monster came into the world with a good heart, but he became cruel after he was rejected by the blind man's family.
		7. Frankenstein was the only one who could create a partner for the monster to solve the problem and stop the terror.
		8. Good inventions may lead to harmful results because of the behavior of people other than the scientist.

GOVERNMENT

Scientists should always be responsible for the consequences of their inventions (Assertion) because _____ (Reason). For example, _____ (Evidence).

REASON	EVIDENCE

OPPOSITION

Scientists should NOT always be responsible for the consequences of their inventions (Assertion) because _____ (Reason). For example, _____ (Evidence).

REASON	EVIDENCE

FORMAT TO DEBATE
Read and learn what to focus on in a rebuttal.

Rebuttals

In order to win a debate, debaters must show that the other side is wrong. The most important way of doing this is through rebuttals. In a rebuttal, you can explain why the other side is wrong. To do this, you should focus on proving that their reasons are wrong. Statements like, "What the other team said is not true," "What the other team said is not always true," "What the other team said is not relevant," and "What the other team said is not significant," help the audience to understand why the other team's argument is wrong.

Debaters should prove that either a reason or evidence is wrong, but it is easier to prove that a reason is wrong or doesn't make sense than to prove that evidence is wrong. Most debaters are careful to use strong evidence, so their evidence will probably not have as many obvious problems. By focusing on reasons, it is possible to find and explain ways that the other team's logic doesn't make sense.

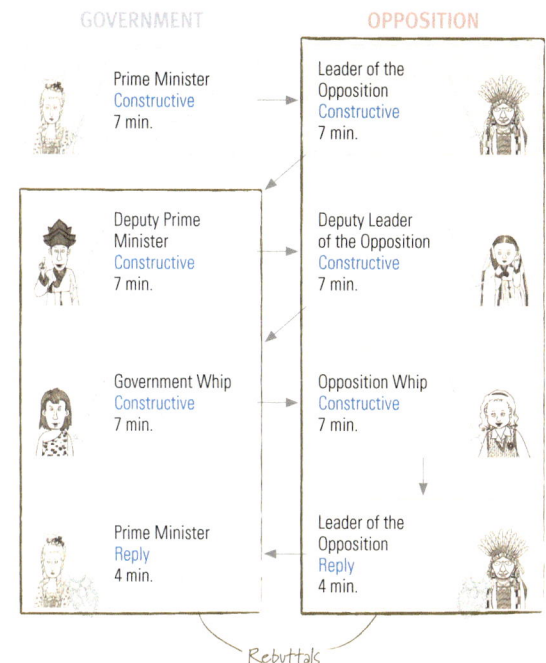

DEBATE KEYNOTES

When giving rebuttals, it is important for debaters to criticize the other team's arguments, but not to criticize the individual speakers of the other team personally.

APPLY TO DEBATE
Choose and write the number for the matching rebuttal next to each reason.

Debate Topic: Scientists should always be responsible for the consequences of their inventions.

REBUTTAL CHAMPION	1. What the other team said is not always true. Other people may be able to share responsibility and help with solutions.
	2. What the other team said is not relevant. Scientists cannot be blamed for all harm.
	3. What the other team said is not relevant. Even if scientists don't predict correctly, they are the only people who can take responsibility.
	4. What the other team said is not significant. Other people can influence an invention, but the scientists have the most responsibility.

GOVERNMENT		OPPOSITION	
Inventions can cause serious harm if scientists make the wrong decision.		Scientists cannot predict how their inventions will turn out in the end.	
Scientists are the best ones to create a solution to problems they create.		Good inventions may lead to harmful results because of the behavior of people other than the scientist.	

DEVELOP TO DEBATE

Insert the reasons and evidence from Argument to Debate into the chart in a logical order. Perform the debate in two groups.

Debate Topic:
This house believes that **scientists should always be responsible for the consequences of their inventions.**

GOVERNMENT

Prime Minister's Constructive [First Affirmative Speech]

DEFINITION This debate argues that scientists should _____ and _____ caused by their inventions. (take the blame for, solve)

TEAM LINE Harm by scientists is real harm. Solutions by scientists are real solutions.

REASON _____ (harm, wrong decision)

EVIDENCE _____

Deputy Prime Minister's Constructive [Second Affirmative Speech]

TEAM LINE _____

REBUTTAL _____ Even if scientists fail to predict correctly, no one else can take responsibility for the results.

REASON _____

EVIDENCE _____

Government Whip's Constructive [Third Affirmative Speech]

TEAM LINE _____

REBUTTAL What the other team said is not significant. Although other people can influence an invention, the scientists who created it in the first place have the first and biggest responsibility.

DETAIL No one forced Frankenstein to _____ It was _____ (create, choice)

Prime Minister's Reply [Affirmative Reply Speech]

TEAM LINE _____

REBUTTAL What the other team said is not significant. If scientists cannot predict the results of their inventions, they should not even dare to create them.

THE BIG PICTURE We believe that _____ because _____ and only scientists _____ (can be very harmful, solve)

98 UNIT 5 LESSON 9 Debate Literature

Debate Format

Asian Parliamentary Debate

OPPOSITION

Leader of the Opposition's Constructive [First Negative Speech]

TEAM LINE We should never punish people for their best work.

REBUTTAL What the other team said is not relevant. Scientists cannot be blamed for all harm, especially if they can't predict it.

REASON

EVIDENCE

Deputy Leader of the Opposition's Constructive [Second Negative Speech]

TEAM LINE

REBUTTAL People who misuse the inventions should share responsibility for the results.

REASON

EVIDENCE

Opposition Whip's Constructive [Third Negative Speech]

TEAM LINE

REBUTTAL What the other team said is not relevant. Scientists should not take blame for what they cannot control.

DETAIL Frankenstein wanted to

but ultimately he _____ (stop, be unable to)

Leader of the Opposition's Reply [Negative Reply Speech]

TEAM LINE

REBUTTAL What the other team said is not significant. Scientists cannot be expected to know the future in detail.

THE BIG PICTURE We do not believe that

because scientists may not be able to

and may not have _____ (predict, cause)

DEBATE CHAMPION TIP

Time in a Parliamentary Debate

In a debate, someone always keeps time for each speech. One student can be the timekeeper and check the time for each speech. The constructive speeches should take almost one minute each, and the reply speeches can take about forty seconds.

LESSON 10: DEBATE CURRENT ISSUES

10A SCHEMA CHAMPION

CRITIQUE TO DEBATE • Free MP3 File Downloadable @www.LARRABEE.co.kr

Read the story carefully, paying special attention to the motives and behaviors of the people involved in the issue.

An Atomic Problem

In August of 1945, then U.S. president Harry S. Truman ordered the military to drop the first two atomic bombs on the Japanese cities of Hiroshima and Nagasaki. Around 200,000 people died, and the two cities were mostly **destroyed**. Fortunately, this is the only time that atomic bombs were used in wartime. Unfortunately, thousands of atomic bombs now exist around the world, creating a strong threat of future use.

The history of the atomic bomb is a major example of the damage that science can do. Many scientists **contributed to** the making of the bomb, and some people say that scientists should solve the problems created by the bomb.

When Albert Einstein discovered the formula $E=mc^2$*, he had no idea that it would lead to such **destruction**. Einstein didn't believe in war and said that fighting in a war was a very unintelligent activity. As Germany, led by Adolf Hitler, became more aggressive, Einstein worried about how the U.S. and Britain would stop Germany's **expansion**.

In 1940, Einstein wrote a letter to then U.S. president Franklin D. Roosevelt. He explained that Germany might create an atomic bomb and that the U.S. should try to develop its own bomb to defend itself from a possible German attack. Einstein strongly believed that Hitler's Germany was an **evil force** that had to be stopped in any possible way.

Roosevelt ordered research into the idea and soon formed the Manhattan Project to develop an atomic bomb. Einstein himself never worked on the bomb, but it could never have been made without his ideas. However, the bomb was not

---

*$E=mc^2$: the theory of relativity; E stands for energy; m stands for mass; c stands for the speed of light; 2 indicates that c is multiplied by itself

ready in time to be of any help in the war against Hitler's Germany.

Five years later, at the beginning of 1945, Germany **was defeated**, and it became clear that the bomb would probably be used against Japan. Many of the scientists working on the project for the U.S. government were upset. One scientist, Joseph Rotblat, even stopped working on the project after Germany was defeated.

Another scientist, Leo Szilard, **arranged to** meet with President Roosevelt to ask him not to use the bomb against Japan. When Roosevelt died, Szilard tried to meet with President Truman. However, he was unable to meet with Truman, and the secretary of state ignored his warnings. This led to the use of two atomic bombs against Japan in 1945.

Since that time, more than six other countries have developed atomic and nuclear weapons. The Cold War in the 1960s, '70s and '80s between the former Soviet Union* and the U.S. has shown that these weapons create fear and terror in every nation, whether or not that nation has atomic weapons.

Beginning in 1945, scientists such as Einstein began to speak out against the bomb. That year, Einstein said that scientists must keep, "warning and warning again," and that they must tell the nations about "the unspeakable **disaster**" they could create. In 1955, two scientists warned that "nuclear bombs can gradually spread destruction over a very much wider area than had been **supposed**" and that a war with these bombs might end all human life. More recently, in 1995, another famous scientist, Linus Pauling, said that all scientists should stop working on projects related to nuclear weapons.

Many people agree that scientists should help solve the problem of these weapons. Scientists often work with scientists in other countries, and these relationships can help to turn any solutions into an international effort. Also, scientists have the knowledge and skills to find ways to make the weapons that already exist less harmful.

Through careful planning and scientific research, the world can become a safer place. This would please Einstein who said after the bombing of Japan, "If only I had known, I should have become a watchmaker."

---

*the Soviet Union: It is also called the USSR (the Union of Soviet Socialist Republics), and it broke into several countries in 1991, including Russia and Ukraine.

CUE TO DEBATE

Discuss the questions. Your answers will be a cue for your debate speech.

Do you think scientists should do more to stop atomic and nuclear weapons?

How do you think these weapons can be stopped?

BUILD TO DEBATE

Study the essential vocabulary for this lesson to build knowledge for debate.

1 LANGUAGE TO COMPREHEND
Choose the correct synonym for each word or phrase.

1. **contributed to** — a. gave something to   b. disapproved of   c. agreed with

2. **expansion** — a. large army   b. strong weapons   c. growth

3. **evil force** — a. place with hard problems   b. something bad with strength   c. something with difficult science

4. **arranged to** — a. hesitated about   b. organized in advance   c. called

5. **disaster** — a. terrible accident   b. natural hazard   c. political problem

6. **supposed** — a. unaccepted   b. well-known   c. expected

2 LANGUAGE TO DEBATE
Choose the correct definition of each word or phrase.

1. Hiroshima and Nagasaki were totally **destroyed** by the dreadful atomic bombs.
   a. hurt completely   b. changed a lot

2. The threat of serious **destruction** from atomic weapons is important.
   a. tragic death   b. complete damage

3. Japan **was defeated** partly because of the atomic bombs dropped by the U.S.
   a. lost completely   b. was hurt

THINK TO DEBATE

Think and share ideas to explore the debatable issues in the story. You may use the cues. You may need to change the form.

1 Why did Einstein write to President Roosevelt about atomic weapons?

• evil force • prevent

2 What happened after the secretary of state ignored Szilard's warning?

• Japan • destruction

3 What were the results of the atomic bombs in Hiroshima and Nagasaki?

• die • destroy

4 How did Einstein react when he found out that an atomic bomb had been dropped in Japan? Why?

• feel responsible • regret

5 What did the Cold War teach us about atomic and nuclear weapons?

• create fear • threat • not have to be used

6 What did Einstein say that scientists should do about atomic weapons? Why?

• warn • disaster

7 Why did Linus Pauling ask scientists not to work on projects related to nuclear weapons?

• peace • more research

8 Why do many people think that scientists should solve the problems of atomic and nuclear weapons?

• knowledge • internationally

**LESSON 10
DEBATE CURRENT ISSUES**

10B DEBATE CHAMPION

ARGUMENT TO DEBATE
Label each part of the arguments. Use "R" for reasons, "E" for evidence, "P" for pro arguments and "C" for con arguments. Then, place the reasons and evidence on the correct side of the debate.

Resolution: Scientists should always be responsible for the consequences of their inventions.

PRO OR CON	REASON OR EVIDENCE	ARGUMENT CHAMPION
		1. Inventions can cause serious harm if scientists make the wrong decision.
		2. Scientists cannot predict how their inventions will turn out in the end.
		3. Good inventions may lead to harmful results because of the behavior of people other than the scientist.
		4. Since Einstein and other scientists did work that led to the atomic bomb, around 200,000 people died in Japan, and two cities were mostly destroyed.
		5. Szilard tried to talk to the president, but the secretary of state ignored him. Thus, two cities were destroyed by atomic bombs.
		6. Einstein believed that his invention would be used to defeat Hitler's Germany, but it ended up causing destruction in Japan.
		7. Scientists have the knowledge, skills and international relationships to find ways to make the weapons that already exist less harmful.
		8. Scientists are the best ones to solve the problems they create.

TEAM A PRO

Scientists should always be responsible for the consequences of their inventions (Assertion) because _____ (Reason). For example, _____ (Evidence).

REASON	EVIDENCE

TEAM B CON

Scientists should NOT always be responsible for the consequences of their inventions (Assertion) because _____ (Reason). For example, _____ (Evidence).

REASON	EVIDENCE

RESEARCH TO DEBATE
Research the following questions to make your argument strong. You may use the cues.

1. Which countries have atomic or nuclear weapons? (countries with nuclear weapons)
2. What happened to the people in Hiroshima and Nagasaki? (aftermath Hiroshima and Nagasaki)
3. Are there good ways to safely destroy nuclear weapons? (how to destroy nuclear weapons)

FORMAT TO DEBATE
Read and learn why rebuttals are important.

Rebuttals

In a rebuttal, debaters present a clash of ideas by refuting the arguments of the other team. Having arguments in direct opposition with each other enhances clash in rebuttals and clarifies each team's point of view.

To make a good rebuttal, you should remember the purpose of rebuttals. Rebuttals help the audience and judges to more clearly understand what the differences are between your side of the debate and that of the other team. In addition to making good rebuttals to show the errors in the other team's arguments, you should choose rebuttals that show how your ideas are distinct from the other team's ideas. They should cover the arguments that are the most opposite, not the ideas with something in common. This makes it easier for the audience to decide which side of the debate they agree with.

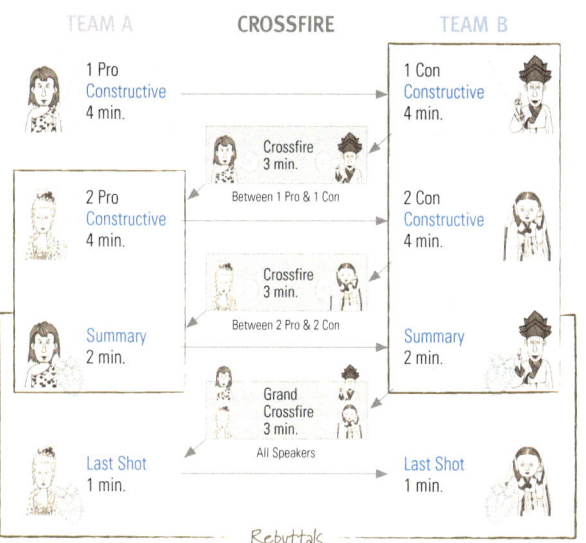

DEBATE KEYNOTES
In Public Forum Debate, the last speaker on each side does not give a rebuttal.

APPLY TO DEBATE
Look at the arguments in Argument to Debate. Choose the two options that show how the two sides are distinct within the debate topic. Then, choose one rebuttal for each team to use.

Debate Topic: Scientists should always be responsible for the consequences of their inventions.

ARGUMENTS
1. The pro side believes that scientists are the only ones with the knowledge and power to change the situation, but the con side believes that other people can change the situation with what they have just like scientists.
2. The pro side believes that the inventions of scientists can be used in harmful ways, but the con side believes that they are not harmful.
3. The con side believes that inventions are used in so many ways that scientists cannot control, but the pro side believes that scientists can control them.
4. The con side believes that scientists feel hurt by their inventions, but the pro side believes that scientists should take control and stop their inventions.

REBUTTALS		
a. What the other team said is not always true. Other people may have the power to share responsibility and create solutions.	PRO	CON
b. What the other team said is not significant. Many people may have caused the problems, but scientists made these problems possible and can change them.	PRO	CON

DEVELOP TO DEBATE

Insert the reasons and evidence from Argument to Debate into the chart in a logical order. Perform the debate in two groups. Instead of a coin toss, Pro team will begin.

> **Resolution:** Scientists should always be responsible for the consequences of their inventions.

TEAM A *PRO* — CROSSFIRE

First Pro Constructive Speech

DEFINITION This debate says that atomic scientists should _____ and _____ (blame for, problems)

TEAM LINE Our world becomes safer when scientists take responsibility.

REASON _____ (wrong decision)

EVIDENCE _____

Second Pro Constructive Speech

TEAM LINE _____

REBUTTAL What the other team said is not relevant. Whatever predictions scientists make, only they can change the results.

REASON _____

EVIDENCE _____

Summary Speech

TEAM LINE _____

REBUTTAL _____ Many people may have caused the problems, but scientists are the root of the problem.

DETAIL President Truman could not have ordered the U.S. to _____ if scientists had not _____ (bombs, create)

The Last Shot

TEAM LINE _____

THE BIG PICTURE We agree that _____

because _____

(harmful OR solve, best)

First Crossfire

Second Crossfire

Grand Crossfire

DEBATE CHAMPION TIP

Real-life Examples
For stronger arguments, give more evidence. You can use evidence from your reading, research or personal experience in similar situations to make your reasons stronger. Since topics are based on current events, periodicals (magazines and newspapers) can also be used for research.

Debate Format

Public Forum Debate

TEAM B *CON*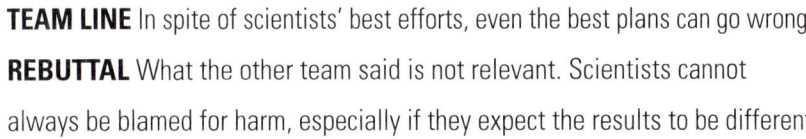

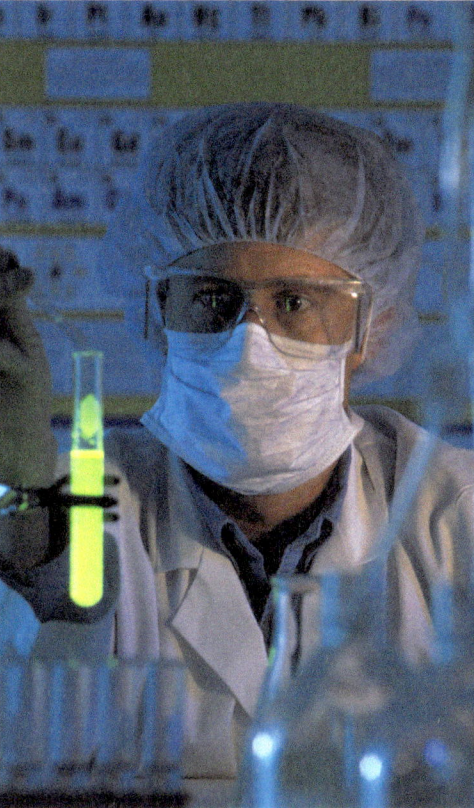

First Con Constructive Speech

TEAM LINE In spite of scientists' best efforts, even the best plans can go wrong.

REBUTTAL What the other team said is not relevant. Scientists cannot always be blamed for harm, especially if they expect the results to be different.

REASON _____ (turn out)

EVIDENCE _____

Second Con Constructive Speech

TEAM LINE _____

REBUTTAL What the other team said is not always true. Other people who misuse inventions may be able to share blame and responsibility and create solutions.

REASON _____

EVIDENCE _____

Summary Speech

TEAM LINE _____

REBUTTAL _____ We should not expect scientists to predict the future in detail.

DETAIL Einstein _____ and wished he _____ (regret his discovery, watchmaker)

The Last Shot

TEAM LINE _____

THE BIG PICTURE We do not agree that _____

because scientists _____
(not predict OR not cause all the problems)

CROSSFIRE TO DEBATE

Write the number of each question by the right speaker. You can also use your own ideas during the crossfire. Take turns to ask and answer completely and politely.

CROSSFIRE CHAMPION

1. Do you think that scientists should not take any responsibility for how others use the scientists' inventions?

2. Don't you think scientists have a responsibility to consider all possible results of their inventions before they create them?

3. Is it reasonable to say that scientists are responsible for harm caused by their inventions even when it happens outside of their control?

4. Why are the scientists' solutions to the problem of atomic and nuclear problems better or more valuable than politicians' solutions?

An Atomic Problem 10B 107

LINK TO DEBATE
Read the situation below. Then, use strong arguments to become a debate champion.

KATHERINE'S DILEMMA

Katherine invented a robot that can wash and dry dishes and stack them neatly on the counter. Unfortunately, she just got a letter from a woman who bought the robot and used it after a dinner party. She charged the robot for one hour, and after the meal, she had the robot wash all the dishes while she visited with the guests. It took more than two hours to wash and dry the dishes, and at the end the robot stopped working properly. It broke her expensive china plates. Katherine feels sorry for the woman. She knows that the woman should have charged the robot for longer, and the robot should not work for more than ninety minutes at a time, though. She doesn't know how to respond to the woman.

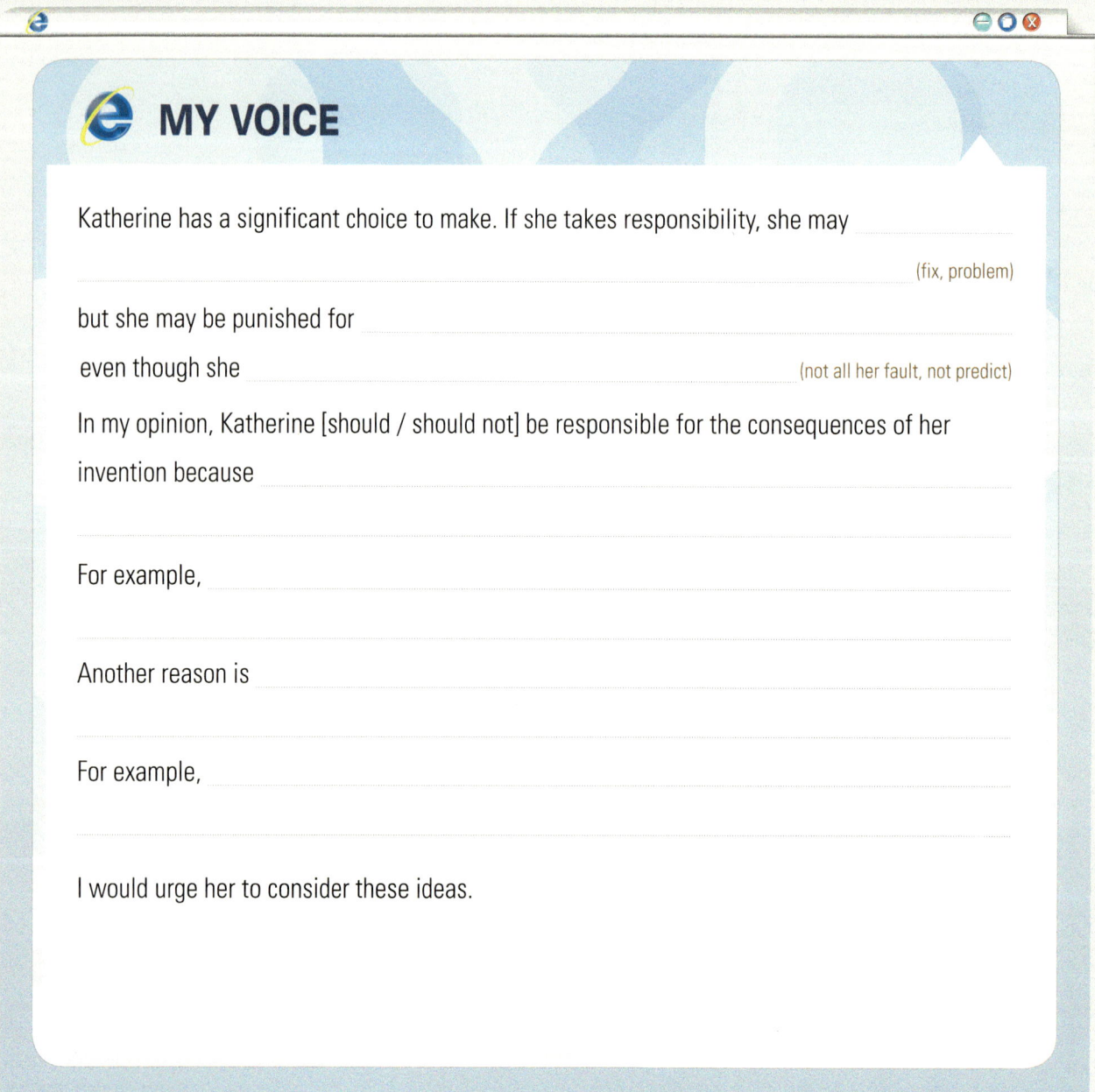

MY VOICE

Katherine has a significant choice to make. If she takes responsibility, she may _____

_____ (fix, problem)

but she may be punished for _____

even though she _____ (not all her fault, not predict)

In my opinion, Katherine [should / should not] be responsible for the consequences of her invention because _____

For example, _____

Another reason is _____

For example, _____

I would urge her to consider these ideas.

UNIT 6: It Is Acceptable to Sacrifice Morals to Gain Money

Our Mutual Friend by Charles Dickens
LITERATURE TO DEBATE

LISTEN TO DEBATE Track 11

Listen and number each box. Take notes while you listen and tell the story using the cues. You may need to change the form.

- dead body
- marry
- Bella
- inherit

- cruel
- run away
- attack
- save

- John Harmon
- love
- Mr. Boffin
- test

- John Rokesmith
- greedy
- die in an accident
- Lizzie

| LESSON 11 | Debate Literature | Our Mutual Friend | Asian Parliamentary Debate |
| LESSON 12 | Debate Current Issues | Quick Cash | Public Forum Debate |

LESSON 11

DEBATE LITERATURE

11A SCHEMA CHAMPION

READ TO DEBATE Track 12

Read the story carefully, paying special attention to the thoughts and behaviors of the main characters.

FACT FILE		
	Context	The story takes place in and around London in the 1850s or 1860s.
	Publication Date	The book was written between 1864 and 1865 in London. It was published one chapter at a time during this time. It was the last novel completed by Charles Dickens.
	Author	Charles Dickens was one of the greatest English writers of the 1800s. He lived from 1812 to 1870.
	Genre	Fiction; Social Commentary

Our Mutual Friend, by Charles Dickens

A young girl and her father floated in a dirty boat on the River Thames. Gaffer Hexam, the father, had found a dead body in the water. He took all the money and papers from the dead man's pockets. Lizzie hated stealing from dead men and complained quietly, but she knew that he only stole to earn money for her and her brother. Gaffer carried the dead man home and called the police. The papers in the dead man's pocket said that he was John Harmon. When the police came to identify the dead man, a young man who called himself Julius Handford followed them. He looked at the body, and then he disappeared.

The story of the dead man was soon well known all across London. John Harmon* had been the son of old Mr. Harmon. Old Mr. Harmon had become rich by digging through piles of trash to find valuable things. In his will, he left all of his money to his son John, but John could only collect the money if he married Miss Bella Wilfer, and he had never even met Bella.

Bella Wilfer lived with her family in a small house. Her father was so kind and pure-hearted that he seemed like an angel. Her mother and sister wanted money more than anything else. They were constantly arguing with each other because Bella's dad didn't earn a lot of money. One day, John Rokesmith, a handsome young man who had just returned to England, came and rented a room in Bella Wilfer's house.

After everyone decided that John Harmon was dead, a loving couple known as Mr. and Mrs. Nicodemus Boffin received old Mr. Harmon's

---

*The main character, John Harmon, has many identities and appears in many parts of the plot that don't seem to be related to each other. The title, *Our Mutual Friend*, reinforces the connection between unrelated parts and characters around him.

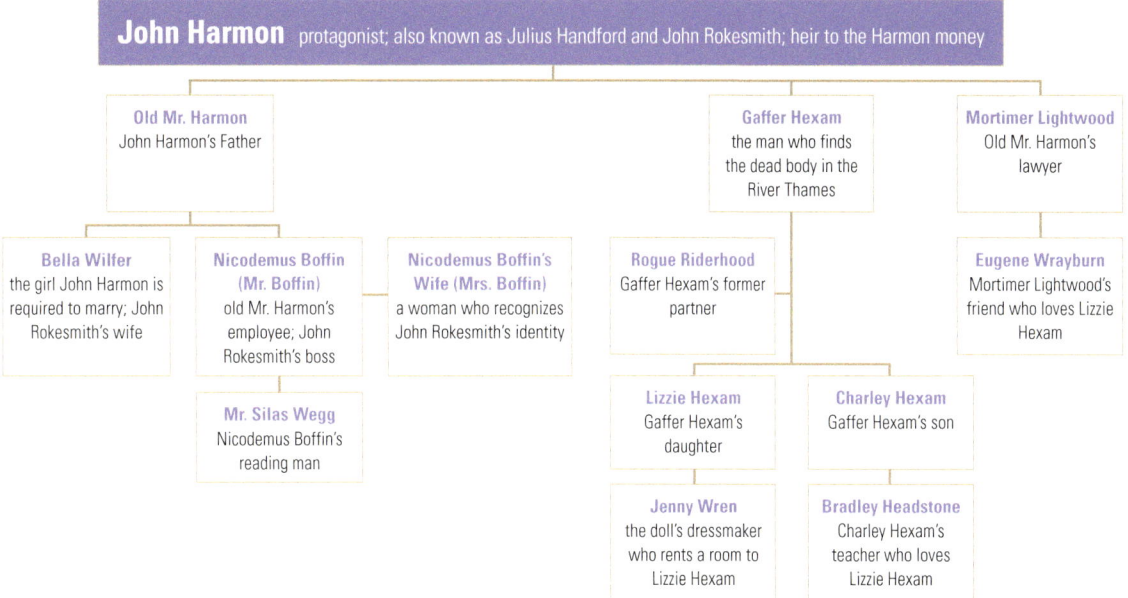

money. Mr. Boffin had worked for old Mr. Harmon, and he had known little John Harmon when he was just a boy. The Boffins were sorry to hear that John Harmon had died, and they felt sorry for Bella Wilfer because she would not become rich by marrying him. So, after Mr. and Mrs. Boffin bought a nice house with the inheritance, they invited Bella to live with them as their **adopted** daughter. Mr. Boffin also hired Silas Wegg to read to him in the evenings, but Wegg couldn't actually read very well.

John Rokesmith heard about Mr. Boffin's money and decided to get a job working for Mr. Boffin. He saw Mr. Boffin in the street and asked him if he needed a secretary. Mr. Rokesmith could write all of Mr. Boffin's letters and help him make decisions about his money. Mr. Boffin hired him, and Mr. Rokesmith proved himself to be an excellent secretary. There was only one strange thing about John Rokesmith. He never talked about his life before he came to London.

Gaffer Hexam didn't want his son Charley to go to school because he never went to school himself. Gaffer couldn't read, and he didn't want his son to read. Charley **desperately** wanted to learn everything, though. One night, before their father got home, Lizzie prepared some things for Charley and told him to go to school.

That same night, Rogue Riderhood, Gaffer's old partner, hoping to get a reward, told the police that Gaffer had killed John Harmon. The police came and prepared to arrest Gaffer, but late into the night, Gaffer's boat still hadn't returned. Finally, the police went out onto the river to search for Gaffer. They found his boat, and under the boat, they found Gaffer. He had been caught in a rope, pulled off the boat and **drowned**. The lawyer in charge of old Mr.

Harmon's money, Mortimer Lightwood, went to tell Lizzie Hexam that her father was dead. His friend Eugene Wrayburn went too.

Lizzie had to leave her father's house and rented a room in the house of a doll's dressmaker. Her brother, Charley, visited her there and brought his schoolmaster Bradley Headstone. Neither of them liked the doll's dressmaker, but Headstone liked Lizzie very much. Eugene Wrayburn also fell in love with Lizzie Hexam and visited her near her new home. Lizzie didn't like either of the men. Headstone asked Lizzie to marry him and told her that Wrayburn would only cause her pain. Hearing this, Lizzie decided to leave London and found a job at a factory.

Meanwhile, Mr. Boffin's secretary, John Rokesmith, fell in love with the beautiful Bella Wilfer. However, Bella only wanted to marry a rich man, and Rokesmith was not rich. Also, Mr. Boffin started to be very mean to Rokesmith. He seemed to distrust Rokesmith. Mr. Boffin also started buying every book he could about stingy men. After a while, Bella became truly afraid that Mr. Boffin had lost all of his kindness.

One day, Mr. Boffin was incredibly mean to Rokesmith. Bella became angry and **confronted** Mr. Boffin with his bad behavior. She declared that if he were to be so selfish, she did not want to **inherit** his money. Bella left and returned to her parents' home. Rokesmith also left and went to look for Bella. Suddenly, Bella realized that she was also madly in love with Rokesmith, and the two of them were soon married.

Silas Wegg, who was living in Mr. Boffin's old house, looked for more treasures in the piles of trash. He found old Mr. Harmon's second will. This will said that the money would go, neither to John Harmon nor to the Boffins, but to the British government. Wegg decided to **blackmail** Mr. Boffin. He would show this will to the lawyer unless Mr. Boffin gave him a lot of money.

After some time, Eugene Wrayburn found out where Lizzie Hexam was living. Wrayburn went to look for her. He didn't know Bradley Headstone was following him. Wrayburn met Lizzie near the river. Lizzie asked him to leave, but Headstone couldn't hear the conversation. He was jealous of Wrayburn and wanted him out of the way. After Lizzie had gone, Headstone **snuck up** on Wrayburn and attacked him. Then, he threw Wrayburn into the river and ran away.

Lizzie, hearing the splash of a body falling into the water, found a boat and sailed quickly to where the body was. She pulled Wrayburn out and screamed for help. Wrayburn was taken to safety, and a doctor came to see him. No one expected him to live, but Lizzie took care of him and tried to make him comfortable. Wrayburn asked Lizzie to marry him, and she agreed, thinking that he would die anyway. They had a small and fast wedding at Wrayburn's bedside. However, Wrayburn didn't die, and Lizzie found that she could live happily with him.

Rogue Riderhood had seen Headstone wearing clothes just like Riderhood's on the day that Headstone attacked Wrayburn. He realized that Headstone wanted to blame him for Wrayburn's murder. Riderhood followed Headstone and attacked him on a bridge over the Thames. They fought desperately, but neither of them could win the fight. Finally, the two men fell, and gripping each other with all their might, they **tumbled into** the Thames.

Finally, Silas Wegg tried to get money from Mr. Boffin by showing him the second will. Mr. Boffin surprised him, though, when he showed him a third will. This third will said that all of the money would go directly to Mr. and Mrs. Boffin. Mr. Boffin finally got rid of Wegg, and that **immoral** man was never seen again.

Bella Wilfer, who was now Bella Rokesmith, finally learned the whole strange story of what had happened between her dear husband and Mr. Boffin. When John Harmon had returned to England to collect his inheritance, he had been robbed. The thief took his clothes and his papers, and then the thief had drowned in the River Thames. This thief was the man who Gaffer Hexam pulled out of the river. The real John Harmon took the name of Julius Handford and saw the dead man's body.

After he knew that people thought he was dead, John Harmon decided to become another man. In this way, he hoped to find out if he could love Bella before he married her and claimed his inheritance. He changed his name again, this time to John Rokesmith. Then, he rented a room at the Wilfer's house to see Bella even better. After she went to live with the Boffin's, he became Mr. Boffin's secretary for the same reason.

One night, he had gone to speak with Mrs. Boffin, and she had recognized him as John Harmon. She knew he was hiding so that he could see Bella better. John Harmon was worried that Bella was too greedy, though, and he wanted to know if she could be happy without money. That is why Mr. Boffin came up with a plan. He decided to act as he was very greedy and be very mean to his secretary. Then, they could see whether Bella would choose Mr. Boffin so as to get his money, or whether she would choose John Rokesmith for love. When Bella had chosen John Rokesmith, everyone had been very happy.

Finally, the true story was known, and John Harmon could claim his own name again. Mr. and Mrs. Boffin gave most of old Mr. Harmon's money to John Harmon and his wife. John and Bella Harmon lived happily together in their magnificent home and had several happy children. They were especially happy when they were visited by Eugene and Lizzie Wrayburn. Mr. Wrayburn had become a much more kind man, and he was truly proud of his poor wife.

Our Mutual Friend, by Charles Dickens

CUE TO DEBATE

Discuss the questions. Your answers will be a cue for your debate speech.

If you were Lizzie Hexam, how would you feel about the way Gaffer Hexam earned a living?

Do you think John Harmon would have married Bella if she had decided to marry for money, not love?

BUILD TO DEBATE

Study the essential vocabulary for this lesson to build knowledge for debate.

1 LANGUAGE TO COMPREHEND
Choose the correct synonym for each word or phrase.

❶ **identify**	a. demonstrate	b. recognize	c. connect
❷ **adopted**	a. grown-up	b. to care for like parents	c. helpful
❸ **drowned**	a. avoided something	b. covered with something	c. killed under water
❹ **confronted**	a. stressed	b. challenged	c. comforted
❺ **snuck up**	a. moved toward secretly	b. stole from	c. ran toward
❻ **tumbled into**	a. hurried around	b. fell into	c. threw something into

2 LANGUAGE TO DEBATE
Choose the correct definition of each word or phrase.

❶ Gaffer Hexam **desperately** had to make money to feed his two children.
   a. hopefully   b. eagerly

❷ Mr. Boffin planned to let Bella **inherit** all of his property.
   a. receive after death   b. take care of

❸ Silas Wegg hoped to **blackmail** Mr. Boffin to get more money.
   a. threaten   b. persuade

❹ Rogue Riderhood was **immoral** and tried to accuse Gaffer of murder.
   a. loud and mean   b. not doing right

THINK TO DEBATE

Think and share ideas to explore the debatable issues in the story. You may use the cues. You may need to change the form.

1. Why were Gaffer Hexam and his daughter in a boat on the river at night?

• steal • make a living

2. How did Silas Wegg lie to Mr. Boffin, and do you think it was wrong? Why or why not?

• educated • not hurt

3. Why did Rogue Riderhood tell the police that Gaffer Hexam killed John Harmon?

• get a reward • money

4. Do you think Bella was more like her greedy mother or her angelic father? Why or why not?

• experience with John and Mr. Boffin • stop caring

5. What happened to Silas Wegg in the end? Why?

• get rid of • morals

6. Why did John Rokesmith wait to marry Bella even after he knew that he loved her?

• not greedy • respect

7. Why do you think Wrayburn didn't regret marrying Lizzie Hexam even though she was poor?

• love • more important

8. Why do you think Mr. and Mrs. Boffin gave John and Bella Harmon most of their money at the end?

• father • happy without money

LESSON 11
DEBATE LITERATURE

11B DEBATE CHAMPION

ARGUMENT TO DEBATE

Label each part of the arguments. Use "R" for reasons, "E" for evidence, "G" for government arguments and "O" for opposition arguments. Then, place the reasons and evidence on the correct side of the debate.

Debate Topic: It is acceptable to sacrifice morals to gain money.

GOVERNMENT OR OPPOSITION	REASON OR EVIDENCE	ARGUMENT CHAMPION
		1. John Rokesmith did not marry Bella right away because he could not respect someone who would only marry to inherit money.
		2. People do not respect people who choose money over morality.
		3. Silas Wegg tried to blackmail Mr. Boffin to get his money, but he lost everything.
		4. Sometimes sacrificing morals is the only way to make a living.
		5. Even though Silas Wegg was immoral and misled Mr. Boffin to earn money, his action didn't hurt anyone.
		6. Without morality, money will ruin your life in the end.
		7. Gaffer Hexam stole from dead people because he desperately had to earn money for his children.
		8. As long as it doesn't hurt others, it's not wrong to choose money over morality.

GOVERNMENT

It is acceptable to sacrifice morals to gain money because _____. For example, _____.
(Assertion) (Reason) (Evidence)

REASON	EVIDENCE

OPPOSITION

It is NOT acceptable to sacrifice morals to gain money because _____. For example, _____.
(Assertion) (Reason) (Evidence)

REASON	EVIDENCE

FORMAT TO DEBATE

Read and learn how to make a good reply speech.

Reply Speeches

Reply speeches are not the same as constructive speeches. They do not include any new assertions, reasons or evidence. They may present some new details about the debate, but their main purpose is to summarize their side of the debate, so they can also be called summary speeches.

In Asian Parliamentary Debate, this speech is given by the same speaker, the Prime Minister, as the first constructive speech. This speaker reviews the information presented so far in the debate and explains it quickly and easily.

The Prime Minister explains to the judges why that team has won the debate. Generally, this means that the speaker will give the team line, a rebuttal and a brief summary. This makes it easy for the audience and judges to remember clearly what has been said in the debate.

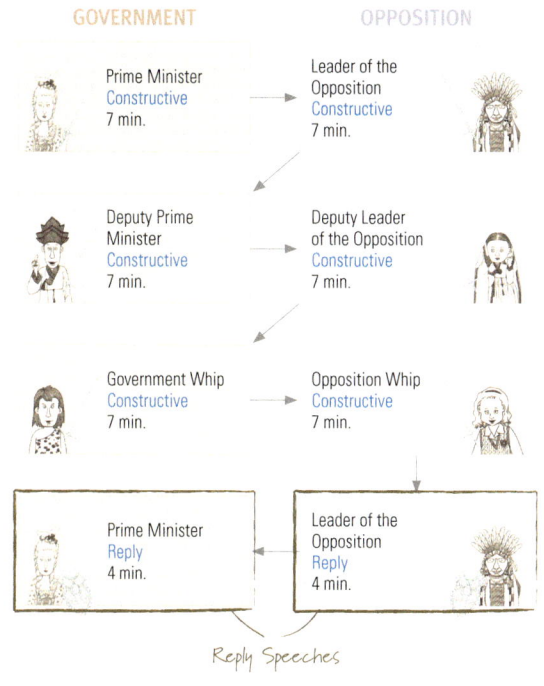

DEBATE KEYNOTES

In a brief summary, it is important for the last speaker on each team to show the audience and judges the big picture of each team's arguments with stronger and more persuasive words.

APPLY TO DEBATE

Choose the sentences to complete the reply speech. There will be one extra sentence that doesn't belong in a reply speech.

Debate Topic: It is always wrong to sacrifice morals for money.

REPLY CHAMPION	1. We do not believe that it is always wrong to sacrifice morals for money because sometimes people need money and have to hurt others to get it. 2. We should not keep people from living a comfortable life. 3. Some people can only get money by sacrificing morals. 4. What the other team said is not true. In some situations, doing the wrong thing is the only choice.

LEADER OF THE OPPOSITION'S REPLY SPEECH

TEAM LINE	
REBUTTAL	
THE BIG PICTURE	

DEVELOP TO DEBATE

Insert the reasons and evidence from Argument to Debate into the chart in a logical order. Perform the debate in two groups.

Debate Topic: This house believes that **it is acceptable to sacrifice morals to gain money.**

GOVERNMENT

Prime Minister's Constructive [First Affirmative Speech]

DEFINITION This debate argues that if people are desperately in need of money, _____
_____ (doing something wrong, better choice)

TEAM LINE It is wrong to deny people a comfortable life.

REASON _____ (make a living)

EVIDENCE _____

Deputy Prime Minister's Constructive [Second Affirmative Speech]

TEAM LINE _____

REBUTTAL _____ People may not even notice when others choose money over morality if it does not affect them negatively.

REASON _____

EVIDENCE _____

Government Whip's Constructive [Third Affirmative Speech]

TEAM LINE _____

REBUTTAL _____ There are many examples of immoral people who lived comfortable lives.

DETAIL Rogue Riderhood would have _____ if he had gotten _____ (easier life, reward from the police)

Prime Minister's Reply [Affirmative Reply Speech]

TEAM LINE _____

REBUTTAL _____ There can be some situations where something that is wrong apparently turns out to be the better choice.

THE BIG PICTURE We believe that _____ because sometimes people must _____ and can get it _____ (money, without hurting)

UNIT 6   LESSON 11   Debate Literature

Debate Format

Asian Parliamentary Debate

OPPOSITION

Leader of the Opposition's Constructive [First Negative Speech]

TEAM LINE If something is wrong, it is always wrong no matter what.

REBUTTAL What the other team said is not true. There is always some other way. Gaffer could have found a job that was acceptable to people in society.

REASON

EVIDENCE

Deputy Leader of the Opposition's Constructive [Second Negative Speech]

TEAM LINE

REBUTTAL Morality does not depend on the situation. Morality is essential for good decisions in the long run.

REASON

EVIDENCE

Opposition Whip's Constructive [Third Negative Speech]

TEAM LINE

REBUTTAL A desire to live comfortably is not a strong enough reason to sacrifice morals.

DETAIL Wrayburn wanted to live well and but after he married Lizzie Hexam, he found that he (rich wife, poor wife)

Leader of the Opposition's Reply [Negative Reply Speech]

TEAM LINE

REBUTTAL People can live a comfortable life without sacrificing morals.

THE BIG PICTURE We do not believe that because it will only (ruin one's life, lose respect)

DEBATE CHAMPION TIP

Longer Constructive Speeches
To make a longer and more understandable constructive speech, try adding a reason. You can choose a reason that is similar to the first reason in the speech to make that reason stronger and more convincing. You can also clarify the reason by paraphrasing it and saying it again another way using more persuasive words.

LESSON 12 DEBATE CURRENT ISSUES
12A SCHEMA CHAMPION

CRITIQUE TO DEBATE
• Free MP3 File Downloadable @www.LARRABEE.co.kr

Read the story carefully, paying special attention to the motives and behaviors of the people involved in the issue.

Quick Cash

In 2008, millions of people could not pay back their **home loans**. This caused many banks to fail and led to the worst international financial crisis* in many years. For years after that, it became difficult for people to find jobs, and prices continued to rise. Many people were unable to **make ends meet**. Desperate to put food on the table, many of these people turned to crime.

Certainly, the connection between economics and crime is not simple. There are many reasons for people to commit crime. People generally steal for one of three reasons. First, some people simply enjoy stealing. They think it is fun to take something without paying for it, and they feel good when they get away with it.

Other people steal because they can make money from it. These professional thieves can go into a store and steal many items. Then, they can sell them on the streets or through other illegal means. They can sell cheaper than the stores because they didn't have to buy them in the first place from a wholesale dealer. This means that they can make more profit than shopkeepers.

A few people steal because they feel like they don't have any other **option**. They may not have enough money at home to survive, and it may be hard for them to buy the things that they need to support themselves. These are the people who are more likely to steal to make a living when the economy is bad. It is easier to understand why these people steal, and yet stealing is considered wrong no matter what the reasons might be.

In every case, stores lose money when people steal. Over time, this means that stores must charge more money to earn the same **profit**. Stealing can cause prices to go up by twenty percent in just two years. For those who are very poor and needy, it is easy to ignore this fact. Prices regularly go up anyway, so it doesn't seem to have much effect. Also, the people who can **afford to** buy the items now will still be able to buy them after the price goes up.

Another crime that becomes more common in difficult economic times is **robbery**. Robbery is taking money or other items from someone who is right there. This is different from stealing,

---

*international financial crisis: a major problem with money and banks in multiple countries at the same time or for the same reason

which is taking things while other people are away or not looking. Usually, people can get a lot more money much quicker through robbery. This is why people often choose robbery when they need to pay large bills like house payments.

Throughout history, these crimes have always been a problem, and hard economic times have been **linked to** many crimes. By comparing bread prices and **crime rates**, it is easy to see that crime rates have risen quickly right after bread prices begin to rise. In fact, the rising cost of bread can help people predict where there might be political problems. People who can't buy bread feel upset with their governments, and they are more likely to start a revolution.

In the end, criminals who rob or steal are very likely to get caught. When they do, they will have to spend time in prison to pay the price for their mistakes. Whatever the reasons are, society cannot and does not accept these types of crime, and criminals will be punished.

As long as the economy is not **stable**, people will feel desperate, and there will be crime. The rising crime rates around the world have shown this to be true. Of course, even in good times, there are a few desperate people and a few greedy people, and there always will be. Crime seems to be a part of our world.

CUE TO DEBATE

Discuss the questions. Your answers will be a cue for your debate speech.

Would you blame someone for stealing food to feed a family? Why or why not?

What would you do to get money if no one in your family could get a job?

BUILD TO DEBATE

Study the essential vocabulary for this lesson to build knowledge for debate.

1 LANGUAGE TO COMPREHEND
Choose the correct synonym for each word or phrase.

1. **home loans** — a. money borrowed for a house b. borrowed houses c. money saved for a house

2. **option** — a. method b. choice c. plan

3. **profit** — a. earnings b. losses c. goods

4. **linked to** — a. fastened to b. connected to c. separated by

5. **crime rates** — a. concern about crime b. speed of stealing c. amount of crime

6. **stable** — a. not dynamic b. depressed c. secure

2 LANGUAGE TO DEBATE
Choose the correct definition of each word or phrase.

1. Many people are not able to **make ends meet** in an unstable economy.
   a. get new things
   b. buy necessary things

2. When people can't **afford to** buy food, they might steal it instead.
   a. have money to
   b. travel to

3. Many people are hurt every year because of **robbery**.
   a. political conflicts
   b. stealing money with a person there

122   UNIT 6   LESSON 12   Debate Current Issues

THINK TO DEBATE

Think and share ideas to explore the debatable issues in the story. You may use the cues. You may need to change the form.

1 What are the three reasons that people steal?

• enjoy • money • not afford

2 Of the three reasons that people steal, which is the most acceptable? Why?

• make ends meet • no other option

3 How does stealing influence the economy?

• profit • raise prices

4 When prices go up because of stealing, why does that hurt people?

• people without much money

5 When are people more likely to rob than to steal? Why?

• economy • amounts • quickly

6 What two changes in society are linked to rising bread prices? Why?

• crime rates • revolutions

7 What happens in the end to people who rob or steal?

• get caught • prison

8 How do you feel about people who steal? Do you or those around you think stealing is ever right?

• wrong • society

12B DEBATE CHAMPION

LESSON 12
DEBATE CURRENT ISSUES

ARGUMENT TO DEBATE

Label each part of the arguments. Use "R" for reasons, "E" for evidence, "P" for pro arguments and "C" for con arguments. Then, place the reasons and evidence on the correct side of the debate.

Resolution: It is acceptable to sacrifice morals to make a living.

PRO OR CON	REASON OR EVIDENCE	ARGUMENT CHAMPION
		1. People look down on those who choose money over morality.
		2. Sometimes sacrificing morals is the only way to make ends meet.
		3. Society disapproves of people who commit robbery no matter what the reason is.
		4. As long as it doesn't hurt others, it's not wrong to choose money over morality.
		5. People who rob and steal will eventually get caught and have to spend time in prison.
		6. Some people steal to get food to put on the table.
		7. Ignoring morality will ruin your life in the end.
		8. Even though prices go up when people steal, other people can still afford to pay the higher prices.

TEAM A PRO

It is acceptable to sacrifice morals to make a living because _____. For example, _____.
(**A**ssertion) (**R**eason) (**E**vidence)

REASON	EVIDENCE

TEAM B CON

It is NOT acceptable to sacrifice morals to make a living because _____. For example, _____.
(**A**ssertion) (**R**eason) (**E**vidence)

REASON	EVIDENCE

RESEARCH TO DEBATE

Research the following questions to make your argument strong. You may use the cues.

1. What percent of people who steal are arrested? (percent of thefts prosecuted)
2. Is the crime rate increasing or decreasing in your area? (change in crime rate [area name])
3. What are the most common crimes in your area? (common crimes list [area name])

FORMAT TO DEBATE

Read and learn what the summary and last shot are.

The Summary and Last Shot

Instead of third constructive speeches and reply speeches, Public Forum Debate uses summary speeches and last shot speeches. Summary speeches give a clear overview of what has happened in the debate up to that point and provide more evidence for their team's view. They also might summarize what was said by the first two constructive speakers.

Because the last shot is the shortest speech, it cannot include much information and does not include any new assertions, reasons or evidence. It generally explains one key argument. This speech should clearly state why the speaker's team's key argument is important and should win the debate. The speaker can explain the argument in a new way or give more examples to strengthen their team's view. Then, everyone can easily remember the most important ideas in the debate and make a good decision.

DEBATE KEYNOTES

A simplified form is used in the Debate Champion series for language learning.

APPLY TO DEBATE

Choose the sentences to complete the speech. There will be one extra sentence that doesn't belong in the speeches.

Resolution: It is always wrong to sacrifice morals to make a living.

SPEECH CHAMPION	1. Wrong actions for a good purpose are acceptable. 2. What the other team said is not always true. In some situations, doing the wrong thing is the only choice to make. 3. This debate says that ignoring morality is always wrong no matter what. 4. We do not believe that it is always wrong to sacrifice morals to make a living because sometimes people need money and have to hurt others to get it. 5. Some people have no other option but to steal to support their family.

SUMMARY SPEECH

TEAM LINE	Wrong actions for a good purpose are acceptable.
REBUTTAL	
DETAIL	

THE LAST SHOT

TEAM LINE	
THE BIG PICTURE	

DEVELOP TO DEBATE

Insert the reasons and evidence from Argument to Debate into the chart in a logical order. Perform the debate in two groups. Instead of a coin toss, Pro team will begin.

> **Resolution:**
> It is acceptable to sacrifice morals to make a living.

TEAM A *PRO* CROSSFIRE

First Pro Constructive Speech

DEFINITION This debate says that if people are desperately in need of money, doing something wrong to _____
_____ (make a living, be a better choice)

TEAM LINE Wrong actions for a good result are not wrong.
REASON _____ (make ends meet)
EVIDENCE _____

First Crossfire

Second Pro Constructive Speech

TEAM LINE _____
REBUTTAL _____

Immorality doesn't change people's opinions of others if it doesn't hurt anyone.

REASON _____
EVIDENCE _____

Second Crossfire

Summary Speech

TEAM LINE _____
REBUTTAL _____

People who live immoral lives often become successful.

DETAIL Most people can easily understand why poor people steal because keeping _____ (morals, not ~ bring success)

Grand Crossfire

The Last Shot

TEAM LINE _____

THE BIG PICTURE We agree that _____
_____

because _____
_____ (a way to earn money OR immoral actions, not always hurt)

DEBATE CHAMPION TIP

Crossfire
For the first two crossfire sessions, debaters stand and face the audience. However, for the grand crossfire session, in which all four debaters participate, debaters remain in their seats, but they still face the audience.